Rich Resmer

4-19-05

Praise for *LESS IS MORE Leadership*

"You won't find this book on my bookshelf. I'll be keeping it on my desk."

BUDDY OWENS—EDITORIAL DIRECTOR,
PURPOSE DRIVEN PUBLISHING

"Dale Burke has written a book that I predict will have significant and lasting success and a lasting impact because it is timeless in its principles and very understandable for those of us who are always looking to improve our leadership skills. I wholeheartedly recommend this book whether you are involved in church, parachurch, government, business, political, or other forms of leadership....This book is priceless."

RON BLUE—CHRISTIAN FINANCIAL
PROFESSIONALS NETWORK

"*LESS IS MORE Leadership* is a grand slam. I have heard Dale speak on this and am cheering him on in the stands. You will not be disappointed!"

DR. GARY ROSBERG—AMERICA'S FAMILY COACHES

"Dale is one of the most remarkable leaders of people I have ever met. He has the uncanny ability to provide visionary guidance and give liberating freedom."

GREG WAYBRIGHT—PRESIDENT,
TRINITY EVANGELICAL DIVINITY SCHOOL

"This is a book every church leader needs to put at the top of their reading list ASAP!"

JIM TOMBERLIN—REGIONAL PASTOR,
WILLOW CREEK COMMUNITY CHURCH

"Dale Burke is first and foremost a practitioner of leadership. He just does it. His experience successfully leading churches of different sizes and shapes confirms that the right principles, properly applied, lead to growth in people and in ministry."

DAN E. MALTBY, PH.D.—PROFESSOR,
MASTERS IN ORGANIZATIONAL LEADERSHIP; DIRECTOR,
THE BIOLA LEADERSHIP PROJECT

"Dale Burke knows firsthand what it's like to tackle an insurmountable leadership challenge, come out on top, and still have a life! Read his book. You'll be glad you did."

LARRY OSBORNE—NORTH COAST CHURCH,
VISTA, CALIFORNIA

"These principles are a tremendous help to balance the demands of life. I apply them extensively myself...and have watched other leaders apply them and gain quality of life and accomplish more as a leader."

STEVE POTRATZ—CEO,
PARABLE CHRISTIAN STORES

"Leading is simple, but it isn't easy. Dale Burke brings clarity to the essential task and helps remove the clutter so that we can do less yet accomplish more."

MARSHALL SHELLEY—EDITOR,
LEADERSHIP MAGAZINE

"Finally! A book on leadership that's supercharged with practical insights, brimming with hope, and rooted firmly in Scripture."

PHIL CALLAWAY—PROFESSIONAL SPEAKER;
AUTHOR OF *GROWING UP ON THE EDGE OF THE WORLD*

"Dale's emphasis on understanding one's greatest contribution and then organizing life around it is truly refreshing. Every leader will benefit from these insights!"

WILLIAM J. HAMEL—PRESIDENT,
ECPA

"The principles in *LESS IS MORE* awaken the desire and provide the pathway for each of us to become healthy servant leaders."

ROB DEKLOTZ—SADDLEBACK CHURCH,
PASTOR IN MATURITY

"For the past nine years I've served on the church staff with Dale. These concepts are in practice daily and create an atmosphere in which every staff member and volunteer flourishes."

DAVE CARDER—AUTHOR OF *TORN ASUNDER:
RECOVERING FROM EXTRAMARITAL AFFAIRS*

"I've watched Dale operate for the better part of 15 years. He knows what he's talking about, and I'm glad he's finally sharing the secret with the rest of us."

JIM SEYBERT—BUSINESS CONSULTANT;
AUTHOR OF *EPM'S GUIDE TO THE CHRISTIAN MARKET*

LESS
IS
MORE
Leadership

H. Dale Burke

Read Again 2012

HARVEST HOUSE PUBLISHERS
EUGENE, OREGON

All Scripture quotations are taken from the New American Standard Bible®, © 1960, 1962, 1963, 1968, 1971, 1972, 1973, 1975, 1977, 1995 by The Lockman Foundation. Used by permission. (www.Lockman.org)

Cover by Koechel Peterson & Associates, Inc., Minneapolis, Minnesota

Published in association with Eames Literary Services, Nashville, Tennessee

LESS IS MORE LEADERSHIP
Copyright © 2004 by H. Dale Burke
Published by Harvest House Publishers
Eugene, Oregon 97402
www.harvesthousepublishers.com

Library of Congress Cataloging-in-Publication Data

Burke, H. Dale, 1953-
    Less is more leadership / H. Dale Burke.
       p. cm.
    ISBN 0-7369-1399-8 (hardcover)
    1. Leadership—Religious aspects—Christianity. I. Title.
    BV4597.53.L43B87 2004
    253—dc22   2004001429

Printed in the United States of America

   04   05   06   07   08   09   10   11   /   DP-MS   /   10   9   8   7   6   5   4   3   2   1

To my greatest leadership mentor and best friend,
Jesus Christ—the source of my hope
that anyone willing to follow His lead
can indeed lead with vision,
love with passion,
and live with joy throughout this journey.
May there be less of me, and more of You,
in all my life and leadership.

Acknowledgments

To the staff and leadership of my church,
First Evangelical Free of Fullerton, California.
Thank you for calling me, trusting me,
and empowering me to lead. You make
LESS IS MORE leadership a joy and
life at the end of the day a reality!

To Steve Miller, and the Harvest House Team.
Thank you for modeling humility and servant-leadership.
You have made me a better writer,
and enabled me to write, lead, and still have a life!
It is a joy to watch you, as a company,
model LESS IS MORE leadership!

To Becky Burke, my wife.
Thank you, sweetheart, for all the respect,
trust, and affection you give me day after day.
You have loved me and encouraged my leadership.
You are my life at the end of the day!

The Leader's Disciplines...

Concentration

Innovation

Imagination

Humility

Spirituality

Humility

Specialization

Mobilization

Determination

©Dale Burke Leadership, 2003

Contents

Every Leader's Dilemma

A Tacoma, Washington, newspaper featured the story of Tattoo, the basset hound. Tattoo hadn't planned to go for an evening run, but when his owner shut the dog's leash in the car door and took off for a drive—with Tattoo still outside the vehicle—the dog had no choice. Fortunately, a motorcycle officer noticed a passing vehicle with something being pulled behind it. It was the basset hound, moving his stocky short legs as fast as he could. The officer chased the car to a stop. Tattoo was rescued and survived, but not before he had reached a speed of 20 to 25 miles per hour and rolled over several times.[1]

When I read that story I thought to myself, *That happens to leaders, too*. You get into a leadership position and you're excited about the joy of leading in ministry or the workplace and before long, you feel as if someone closed the car door on your leash and took off—not intending to drag you along. And all you can do to survive is run as fast as your little basset hound legs can go!

I love the story about Tattoo. I love the fact he was a basset hound with short, stubby legs and not a Great Dane. Can you picture his legs just churning furiously? He had probably never run that fast before, but he had no choice because he was running for his life.

As a leader, I can identify with Tattoo on so many levels:

Someone else is holding the leash.

Life is out of my control.

I'm just one small dog.

The car is too big and too strong.

It's run or be run over.

Nobody asked me.

Survival is the goal.

The driver is clueless about my condition.

I feel like "biting" the guy behind the wheel!

At times I feel as if forces beyond my control have me on a leash—as if the demands of both life and leadership have grabbed me by the neck and are pulling me down the street before I'm ready to go for "a ride," let alone go for "a run" just to keep up! Tattoo never had a vote or choice. His only option was to run or die. So he ran...and by the grace of God and the goodness of Officer Filbert, he survived so we could read his story, and not his doggie obituary! We can be sure that for Tattoo, life felt out of control and unfair.

I have felt that way many times as a leader at a large church. I'm working hard just to keep up. I'm trying to get on top of the pile before I'm buried by it. I'm trying to survive this week and get through another Sunday, hoping next week will be a little less intense or a little less busy. But the reality is, by the time next week comes, I'm as busy as ever. As a friend once said, for a pastor, it seems Sunday comes every three days!

Leading, but Always Feeling Behind!

Leaders everywhere—in corporations and churches of all sizes—are feeling the rush. When I ask them to describe their life, they tend to use three words: I am *busy*, *buried*, and *behind*. I've heard this so much that I now call this sense of being overloaded "the B-Zone." Not only do we say, "I am busy," or "I am buried," but also...

I feel *broke*. I never have enough money
to do what I want to do.
I feel *blocked*. My fellow leaders or my circumstances
won't cooperate with me.
I feel *bugged*. The same problems keep coming up
again and again.
I feel *bummed*. At times it's
downright depressing.

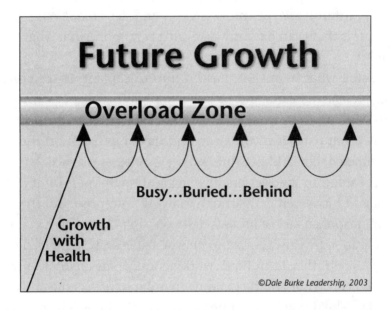

Future Growth

Overload Zone

Busy...Buried...Behind

**Growth
with
Health**

©Dale Burke Leadership, 2003

If you have felt those emotions too, I have good news for you. After 25 years of leading three different ministries, ranging in size from 28 members to over 5000 members, though I've been in that B-Zone, I'm still having fun! Leadership and life are indeed a challenge, but you can lead, pursuing your dreams with gusto, and still have a life. I know. Let me add one more "b" word to the list...

I feel *blessed!*

Why? Because I now know from experience it's possible to lead and still have a life. Visionary leaders are not required to always be busy,

What about
Task

buried, and behind and sacrifice their marriages, families, and personal health on the altar of success. There is a better way—a way to both lead *and* live with real joy.

The Leader's Dilemma: What Will I Sacrifice?

I was in the office of an attorney who expressed an interest in *LESS IS MORE Leadership*. As we discussed the eight core concepts we're about to explore together in the upcoming chapters, he leaned forward in his chair, interrupted me mid-sentence, and declared, "What you're telling me is that I can have my cake and eat it, too. Is that what you're saying?"

Not sure what he meant, I asked him to explain. He responded, "Well, ever since I came out of law school, joined the law firm, and entered the corporate race, I wanted to win. I wanted to be successful, become a full partner in the firm, and have my name on the door. So I competed, ran, and I've finished the first leg of the race. My name is on the door, in gold letters. I've made some money, built a reputation, and I love being a part of a growing enterprise. But from day one, an unspoken fact of life was that you can't have it all if you want to be a leader. I've always had to choose between being a leader and having a life. Either I run hard, working longer and harder to win at work, or I check out and head home in order to have a life at the end of the day. The prevailing assumption is that it's impossible to do both. The choice was simple: Which would I sacrifice today? I've always struggled with that choice. But what you're telling me is that God's design for leadership makes it possible for me to pursue both at the same time. That personal health and professional success are not mutually exclusive. I can lead with vision, pursue my dreams, and still enjoy life. I can have my cake and eat it too."

The attorney was right on target. Balancing life and leadership is tricky business, but it can be done. Leaders can be visionary dreamers and still sleep at night! The road to professional success can also lead to great personal satisfaction on the home front.

Yet in every arena of leadership today, I encounter leaders who feel the tension expressed by the attorney above. How to lead and still have a life is a challenge faced by every leader who truly wants to lead with excellence. No matter when and where you lead, leadership is tough, and it's getting tougher. And the stress is being felt by leaders at every level. The common assumption is that the solution is to pray harder, work harder, and work longer hours. As a result, leaders today are being stretched until they snap under the pressure of today's fast-paced, high-demand, rapid-change culture. They eventually hit a crisis point at which the health of the leader and organization begin to go downhill. The reality is that praying harder, working harder, and working longer hours is not the answer.

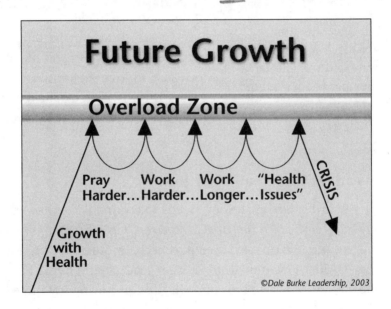

©Dale Burke Leadership, 2003

The High Calling of Leadership

As you may know, my personal leadership experience is not in the corporate world, but in ministry. I am the senior pastor of a large Southern California church with over 5000 members. And of course, leadership in real life is always more than a job. My leadership resumé includes other very important elements:

Dale Burke
Person with a Life
Husband of One Wife
Father of Three
Pastor of 5000

All of us need to realize leadership is more than a job or career. It is a calling of the highest order. In each arena of our life, we are called to lead. In each aspect of our leadership, we are to be the best leader we can be. We are to lead ourselves toward maturity as children of God who were created by Him to live for His glory. We are to be a lover-leader in our marriage till death do we part. We are to lead our children to become healthy young adults ready to lead and love life, and prepared to face their own life-challenges and carry on a legacy worthy of reproduction.

> ⟨⟨⟨ ⟩⟩⟩
>
> "*Overload* reminds us of the weight of everyday life. We are overwhelmed, over-worked, overcommitted, overanxious, overmatched and overextended. Our tanks are on empty and we're running on fumes."[2]
>
> —STEVE AND MARY FARRAR

Every Leader: Three Full-time Jobs

Maybe your leadership resumé reads like mine. *The personal side of my life could easily be a full-time job: person, husband, and father.* If I were wealthy and had no need for a paycheck, I would have no trouble investing 40, 50, or even 60 hours a week leading and living my personal life, loving and caring for my wife, and nurturing my three kids to be all that God wants them to be. As a leader who wants to have a life, I cannot ignore the demands of everyday life.

For example, my spouse wants and needs a piece of my time, attention, and energy. I learned years ago, "If mama ain't happy, nobody's happy!"; at least not for long. Then you add kids to the mix. What a joy! But also, what a job! Keeping up with all those lessons, shuttling them here and there, and just trying to fulfill the role of mom or dad can be exhausting. The Little League needs an assistant coach. The school needs a "room mom" or "room dad." There are parent-teacher conferences or it's a new quarter with another "back to school" night. The Rotary Club wants me for their community project and the church will shut down one of my kid's Sunday school class if someone doesn't volunteer to teach. And what about me? I really need some personal time just reconnecting with my friends—or being alone. Add to the list the date night my wife and I said we would always do once a week to keep our marriage alive and refreshed! See what I mean? Just living life could be my full-time occupation.

> *Every career for the man or woman following Christ is a divine calling—an assignment from heaven, a part of God's grand design for your life.*

But that's not reality for me, and most likely, the same is true for you. The bills have to be paid. There is a job to report to daily. And even if I didn't need a paycheck, I'd still need something to do! Every career for the man or woman following Christ is a divine calling— an assignment from heaven, a part of God's grand design for your life. Work was never intended to simply be a distraction on the way to the weekend! It is not a "necessary evil." Even before the fall of mankind in the Garden of Eden, God gave Adam and Eve work to do. They cared for the Garden. Work is not the result of sin, as some people think. It only got harder after the fall.

We were created to work, but we were also created to rest, to relate, and to walk with God, as explained in the sidebar on this page. And at the center of all our working, resting, and relating is worship—our relationship with our Creator. In fact, our relationship with God, as we will explore later, can and should be a vital component that empowers our work, enriches our rest, and improves every relationship in our life. So we must learn to lead in the workplace and still have a life. If we don't get a strong handle on the demands of leadership, we can lose our grip on life itself.

My job, like yours, can be demanding. I work full time for a "branch of a global enterprise" called the church, whose mission is to change the world and take the Founder's message to every person alive. *So I*

>>> **God's Design for Us** <<<

《《〈 〉》》

God's Design for Us

Genesis 1:27—*worship:* "God created man in His own image"

Genesis 2:15—*work:* "God took the man and put him into the Garden of Eden to cultivate it and keep it"

Genesis 2:3—*rest:* "He rested from all His work"

Genesis 2:18—*relate:* "it is not good for the man to be alone"

must stay visionary, mission-focused, and growth-oriented as a leader. Mere management—the maintenance of "what is"—will not satisfy my "leadership soul" nor please the heart of my CEO, Jesus Christ. He loves people and wants the church to "go therefore and make disciples of all the nations" (Matthew 28:19). That's a full-time job that can easily demand every ounce of energy and creativity I can muster!

But that's not all I'm called to do as a pastor-leader. *My job description also challenges me to care for the needs of my church members* in the same way that a loving shepherd watches over a flock of sheep. I'm to serve them, feed them, comfort them, marry and bury them...all 5000-plus of them! And these sheep get hungry and demand to be fed. They hurt and demand to be comforted. They get sick and need a vet now, not later. Does that sound like your customers or employees?

Just managing "what is," or caring for your people or today's customers, can be a full-time job. You see, whether we are growing a church, or expanding a business, or educating a classroom of students, every leader must manage the present while going after the future, or eventually there will be no future at all. So count it up—that's three full-time jobs for any leader who wants to lead and live in the way God designed for us to live.

- The leader must maintain his or her personal life—staying spiritually and personally fit while meeting the needs of his or her family.

- The leader must maintain "what is"—serving and caring for his members, customers, and employees.

weakest here.

3

- Yet the leader must also pursue "what could be"—reaching forward and advancing the mission of the church or company God has entrusted to the leader's care.

So how do you successfully juggle the demands of life and leadership? You may be surprised to know that it's not about doing *more*, but *less*. Adding is not the answer. Faster is not the answer. When it comes to succeeding as a leader and in life, less is more.

> *Everything in our culture seems to work against winning both at work and in life.*

What Every Leader Needs to Know

To lead bigger, one must lead smarter. Effecting change, chasing new dreams, seeking to grow healthy families, building bigger fortunes, or advancing faith-based ventures all require smart leadership. Moving anything toward excellence in today's world of mediocrity is challenge enough. When I add the desire to lead and *live well*—with real joy in every dimension of my life resumé—the task can seem overwhelming. Everything in our culture seems to work against winning both at work and in life. Yet I'm here to say that it *can* be done. How can I be so confident? Because of Christ's example and the Father's care.

?
/

Had no wife + kids!

Jesus Christ is the ultimate model for leadership with a life. He was a winner, both in the pursuit of His mission and His personal life. He was, by all standards, history's greatest leader. Furthermore, as He launched His movement, He challenged His "executive team" to dream big, be visionary, and go global, yet He also promised them full joy and abundant life at the same time. Quality of life was so important to Jesus that leaders in His organization would be judged not only by their "customers and accounts" (converts), but by their "character" (life at the end of the day). In fact, a failure to "live well" could even disqualify one from leadership in his new "company," the church. That's why the apostle Paul took the time to explain clearly the character qualities that should be part of a spiritual leader's life. While these qualities have church leaders in mind, they're valuable for those in the corporate world too.

Our heavenly Father understands us. He knows you and me better than we know ourselves. And on top of His incredible understanding, He loves us and proved it in history with the greatest gift, the most incredible sacrifice of love ever given. We often listen to what He says about life; perhaps it's time we listen to what He says about leadership. He is the ultimate leadership guru.

The chapters you are about to read will unfold, step by step, eight disciplines for being a leader and still having a life. These disciplines are gleaned from Jesus' example as a leader over a worldwide venture. The eight core principles were each taught and modeled by Jesus and then reaffirmed in the leadership manual for the early church. And when they are followed, they lay a sure foundation for effective, visionary leadership as well as a balanced, joyful life.

These eight principles work because they are Truth with a capital T. They transcend the ebb and flow of modern trends and fads. Modern leadership research often discovers and reinforces them, but never can begin to replace them. These principles empower effective leadership and can be applied wherever you lead: at home, at work, or at church. Good leadership always involves these eight, and we're going to discover how we can make them real in our lives. They will help you to lead effectively...and still have a life.

The Inner Ring—the Heart of the Leader

Spirituality	The Power of Convictions
Humility	The Power of Servant-leadership

The Middle Ring—the Heart of Leadership

Imagination	The Power of Vision
Mobilization	The Power of Letting Go
Specialization	The Power of Unique Abilities
Innovation	The Power of Creativity

The Outer Ring—the Heart of Execution

Concentration	The Power of Focus
Determination	The Power of Hope

©Dale Burke Leadership, 2003

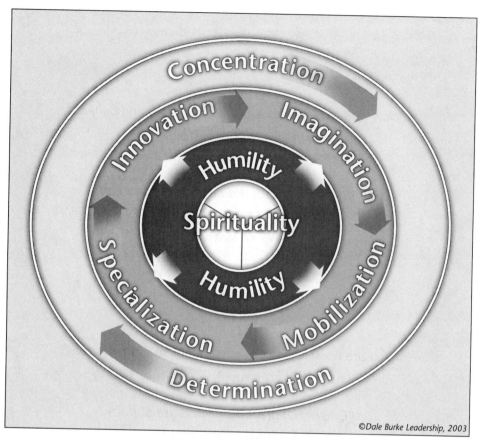

©Dale Burke Leadership, 2003

8- Disciplines
For Leaders

"How do I feel? Three words: busy, buried, and behind."
—FROM A SURVEY OF PASTORS AT A
LESS IS MORE LEADERSHIP SEMINAR

*"Ten more minutes. I'd be thrilled if you can
just give me ten more minutes per day."*
—VP OF MARKETING

"Ruthlessly eliminate hurry from your life."
—DALLAS WILLARD,
AUTHOR AND PHILOSOPHER, USC

"You are worried and bothered about so many things."
—JESUS CHRIST TO A BUSY MARTHA (LUKE 10:41)

*"One of the great disadvantages of hurry
is that it takes such a long time."*
—G.K. CHESTERON IN *ALL THINGS CONSIDERED*

CHAPTER ONE

Ten Undeniable Facts
for Today's Leaders

It's a tough time in which to be a leader. Leaders today face diffi-
culties that can perplex the veteran and surprise the beginner. It's as
if, just when we learned the game, someone changed the rules.
Expectations and demands have risen to an all-time high. For many,
it is a "do more on less, or else" world. For others, what worked in
the past just isn't getting the job done anymore. Virtually all leaders
are feeling busy, buried, and behind with a to-do list that's much longer
than their day.

Peter Drucker, a respected business guru who tracks societal shifts,
wrote,

> Every few hundred years in Western history, there occurs a
> sharp transformation....Within a few short decades, society
> rearranges itself—its worldview, its basic values, its social and
> political structure, its arts, its key institutions. Fifty years later,
> there is a new world. And the people born then cannot even
> imagine the world in which their grandparents lived and into

which their own parents were born. We are living through
just such a transformation.[1]

In the past, yesterday's successes provided the wisdom for
tomorrow's leaders. What worked in the past was copied, printed, dis-
tributed, and applied in the present. Success trickled down as our managers, mentors, and elders passed on their methods and techniques
to the next generation. As time went on, however, leaders came to
realize the old approaches were not producing the same results. Things
had quietly, almost mysteriously, changed. Leaders responded by
working harder, longer, and even muttering a prayer or two as they
did. They were busy, buried, and falling further behind. They worked
harder than ever, with little to show for it. It worked before, but why
not now? Reflect on a parable with me:

> Once upon a time there was a great lake. It was deep and wide and
> a source of great joy for many who grew up on the shores of the
> lake and explored its waters in their canoes. The local residents
> enjoyed getting out of their canoes to float or swim in the cool
> waters. Occasionally a novice or non-swimmer would drown, but
> the local residents learned to make sure everyone at least knew how
> to swim to shore. Life was good on the lake.
>
> One day the great dam that made the lake possible developed a
> leak. The leak slowly but surely drained the beautiful lake. Even-
> tually the residents awoke one day to find not the lake, but a river.
> The river had always been there, but out of sight. It was the source
> of the water that had formed the lake.
>
> The river carried the same volume of flow, the same cool water as
> it always had. Yet without the dam, it was very different. As the
> boaters took to the river, many were surprised at its power and
> strange currents. Even good canoers struggled to go where they
> wanted to go. The lake had been manageable, but the river was a
> different story. Good swimmers soon learned that floating with this
> current could be fatal. And those who jumped overboard to refresh
> themselves in the water did so with tragic consequences. After a
> season, most of the people who had once enjoyed the lake chose

to stay on the safety of the shore. They avoided the dangerous water—yet in doing so, they also avoided the joys of the water.

Leaders today face a far greater challenge than their counterparts a few decades ago. Whether you are trying to lead a church or a corporation, it is a different world and a tougher time in which to be a leader. Every leader knows this, but few know what to do about it. It's time for a new plan for rafting the river. Twenty-first-century leaders must bid farewell to the good old days on the lake and now must lead through the rapids.

The safety of the shore is not even an option for most; it is sink or swim. Yet Christian leaders need not despair at the sight of the river or the unknown challenges ahead. Like a great rafting river, it holds both great peril and great promise. It is, at the same time, both dangerous and delightful, offering both challenges and opportunities.

> *"Some leaders have 20 years' experience, and others have one year of experience repeated 20 times!"*

The leader's trusted tool is no longer the map of the lake, for the lake is gone. For this new journey the leader needs a compass and a sextant, or in today's world, a GPS device! A leader must know how to pinpoint his or her current location, and be skilled charting the next steps forward.

Without clear direction, many leaders merely waste their energy. Like a panicked swimmer gone overboard, they beat the water and quickly tire out with little or no real progress to show for their effort. They are indeed busier than ever, only to discover they have been going in circles. They merely repeat their past and call it progress. Dr. Howard Hendricks, a longtime friend and mentor, once said to me, "Some leaders have 20 years' experience, and others have one year of experience repeated 20 times!"

The eight principles of *LESS IS MORE Leadership* are designed to make sure that can never be said of you. But before we look at those principles, we must answer a couple of key questions: Why are we so busy, buried, and behind? And why do past formulas for success no longer work today?

Ten Facts of Life for 21st-Century Leaders

1. The Rules Have Changed
2. Life Is Faster
3. Change Is Accelerating
4. Expectations Are Higher
5. The Culture Is in Moral Decay
6. Servant-leadership Is Stretching
7. You Are a Limited Resource
8. Leadership Is a Draining Experience
9. More Is Not the Answer
10. There Is Hope

Ten Facts of Life for 21st-Century Leaders

1. The Rules Have Changed

Peter Drucker was right when he said we're living through a time of transition. Our society now thinks by a different paradigm and accepts a radically different set of assumptions about themselves, their lives, morality, and especially spirituality. To ignore these changes and lead as if we were still in the first half of the twentieth century is a deadly mistake. It is indeed like trying to navigate the rapids in a rowboat made for the lake. These changes are so many they could fill a book.

Worldview Shift

- The Christian worldview, which used to dominate the thinking of American culture, believes people are created in the image of God. Today's culture, by contrast, believes we are one more link in a long evolutionary chain of cosmic accidents.

- The Christian worldview believes there is life after death and that every person will be held accountable for his or her choices on earth. Our culture believes either that we only go around once in life, so grab for all the gusto you can get, or that eternity is a joyful bliss for all, regardless of what we do here on earth.

- The Christian worldview believes that moral absolutes, right and wrong, exist to help protect us. Our culture believes all morality is relative and only right or wrong for the individual. The post-modern Great Commandment is "whatever."

- The Christian worldview believes that truth is available and worthy of pursuit. Our culture believes truth does not exist or is unknowable because it is always the result of each person's environment.

- The Christian worldview believes that God is real, personal, loving, and most importantly, wants a relationship with people like you and me. Therefore the Divine is not silent, but has spoken. Our culture believes God might exist, but is at best a mystery, silent and unknown.

- The Christian worldview believes God is eternal, unchanging, and that He created man in His image. In today's culture, each person imagines his own "god." To the twenty-first-century skeptic, God—if he, she, or it exists at all—is "made in our image" to be what we want him, or her, to be.

The environment in which we lead has been radically altered. Do you see how the lake has become a river? Just a few decades ago, Judeo-Christian values and a Judeo-Christian worldview dominated the thinking of the American masses, no matter what their personal faith.

Being a leader in such a world was a challenge, but not nearly as hazardous as it is today. For us to try to lead as if the world hasn't changed would be like launching into the biggest rapids on the Colorado River in a canoe made of toothpicks!

2. Life Is Faster

The pace at which life is being lived today is brutal. It's hard to keep up, and when we choose to run with the masses, we only end up killing ourselves. How fast is it? I read a story reported in *Newsweek* magazine about the city of Ridgewood, New Jersey.[2] The town was featured because the people there decided to set aside one day for everyone to rest and just be together as families. No soccer, no baseball, no activities, no conferences, no school meetings, no homework. This day of rest ended up getting the town into a national magazine! Now, they didn't set aside a day a week; they set aside just *one day*. Even one day can help in the struggle to restore balance to their busy lives. Too often we keep living at such a harried pace that our busyness ends up having a negative effect on everything we do as leaders. The same is true whether you are a leader in ministry or in the marketplace. Life is faster, and leaders dare not ignore that. This small town, however, discovered less can be more, and we need to make the same discovery.

3. Change Is Accelerating

Rapid changes are taking place in both the marketplace as well as in ministry. What worked yesterday used to have a lifespan of "X" number of years. Whatever that "X" factor was yesterday, it has become a lot shorter today. That's just the reality of the world in which we live, and it puts more pressure on leaders to stay on top of their game.

This reality is faced by every inventor, every entrepreneur, every professional or pastor. Products and services must change or soon end up without buyers. Churches must adjust, or the pastor will soon speak to a graying audience with no younger generation for the future. Yet how are we to stay "on the edge" without falling "off the cliff"? We will explore this tension, and its solution, later on in our LESS IS MORE principles for managing change.

4. Expectations Are Higher

People have higher expectations than ever before—in both the business world and in churches. This includes everything: what they expect from the church nursery, what they desire from the worship services, how the youth ministry addresses the tumultuous world of their teens. Expectations are up for every church that wants to be in business, let alone really flourish.

And ministry and the marketplace are not as different as you might think. The bottom line for both is service to survive—to please or perish. I have customers, and so do you. And if my customers don't like the product that they're getting, there are many other places they can go for the same product. And they are very quick to find a new spiritual outlet to meet their needs.

Studies have been done recently, for example, on denominational loyalty. It used to be that when people moved to a new city, a Methodist would go to a Methodist church, a Presbyterian would go to a Presbyterian church, a Catholic would go to a Catholic church, and so on. Whatever your background, that's where you went to church. It didn't matter all that much if the church wasn't all that good.

But that's no longer true. These days, people shop for the church that best serves the needs of their family. And they will go to the one they feel fits them best regardless of the denominational affiliation. The same is true for businesses. People are loyal only for as long as all their needs are met. Expectations are higher, and that affects every one of us who tries to be an effective leader.

> ⟨⟨⟨⟩⟩⟩
>
> "It doesn't matter what you did last week to justify your employment; 'what have you done for me lately?' is the ongoing question within a competitive workplace environment. Capitalism really is natural selection in action."
>
> —JEFF KEY, REAL ESTATE AND FINANCIAL ANALYSIS

5. The Culture Is in Moral Decay

Moral decay not only affects church leaders, its impact is felt by leaders in every segment of society—especially the business world. We're all dealing with employees and customers, partners and peers, who are coming out of a confused culture that is in a state of moral decline. *The rules have been rewritten and the number one rule is there are no rules.* Except, perhaps, this one: Don't get caught! "Business ethics" has joined the list of oxymorons such as jumbo shrimp and almost perfect. The corporate scandals of the last decade have unveiled the lack of integrity and honesty previously reserved for political and religious scandals of a decade ago or so.

This decay affects every leader because at the heart of every church, business, or team is people. People are the stuff of which your organization is made. Like parts of a machine, low-quality components mean a low-quality machine. Maintenance goes up. Productivity goes down. It is a fact of life. So it is with the business of leading people. Yet this is your world, and these are your people. God has called you to serve and lead them.

Today, we lead in a world that's confused and searching for answers. Brokenness and addictions are so commonplace that they feel like the norm. Every time a member of your church or company goes through a divorce, struggles with a child on drugs, has an affair, contracts a disease, becomes clinically depressed, or simply decides it is now okay to lie, you as a leader catch the fallout. LESS IS MORE Leadership, as you will read in the next chapter, calls leaders to make sure they themselves are stable so they can lead and live well in this morally unstable world.

6. Servant-leadership Is Stretching

Most Christians today affirm a desire to follow the challenge of Jesus to be a "servant-leader." Even the business community recognizes the benefit of servant-leadership. Jim Collins's bestselling book on corporate leadership, *Good to Great,*[3] acknowledges from a secular research perspective that having a humble spirit or a servant approach to leading in business actually helps you succeed. We'll see why when we explore the power of humility later in this book.

While being a servant-leader is great, it also stretches us. It requires a dual focus by the leader and creates what I call the *servant-leader tension.* Now in a general sense the tension that's felt in the ministry is different than the tension felt in the marketplace. But at the core, they're both the same. Let me explain, first by sharing from my role as a pastor.

When Jesus picked His first followers, He was choosing the leadership team who would launch the church. These small groups of men and women were to lead the charge to plant the church not just locally, but globally. Global outreach and growth was, and remains today, a key component of the mission and mandate for the church. Yet their leadership style was to be different than that found in secular culture. How different? Listen to His leadership training presentation:

> "You know that the rulers of the Gentiles lord it over them,
> and their great men exercise authority over them. It
> is not this way among you, but whoever wishes to be first
> [great] among you shall be your servant" (Matthew 20:25–26).

According to Jesus Christ, great leaders are servant-leaders. They love their people enough to get down and dirty with them. They don't lead from the tower; they get down in the trenches. They serve and empower their people. They use their influence and resources to knock down barriers, remove obstacles, and enable those serving under them. That's servant-leadership.

And then Jesus challenged His key leaders, saying, "Here's your mission." Listen to their corporate assignment:

> "Go therefore and make disciples of all the nations,
> baptizing them in the name of the Father and
> the Son and the Holy Spirit" (Matthew 28:29).

Now can you imagine starting a global company or mission from scratch, with just a dozen or so potential "branch managers"? And these future leaders didn't even have churches to lead. The church had yet to be born! The clear mandate was not maintenance, but mission—to grow and expand the kingdom of God.

So, on the one hand they were to be servants, yet on the other hand they were to take charge and grow the company, expand the organization, enlarge the operation. Jesus commissioned them to establish branch offices in every single nation of the world. Now, He didn't

If all you do is care for the present, eventually you will die.

tell them they could take the next 3000 years to establish His work globally. He didn't give them any time frame. He just laid out the mission and said, "I want you to go for it."

Do you see the tension created by those two commands from Jesus? The first command tells us to be a servant, to care for our people. This could easily require all of our time and energy. Even in the first church I pastored, which had about 50 or 60 members, there were enough personal needs in people's lives that I could spend all of my time just caring for them, discipling them, equipping them, and helping them discover how to live life, have a good marriage, raise their kids, love, serve, and worship their God. Just serving people, being a servant, is always a full time job.

At the same time, I could have easily given all my time, energy, and attention to fulfilling Jesus' second command—go out, reach more people, and grow the church. So in a real sense, Jesus has given every leader in the church two full-time jobs: 1) care for the flock, and 2) go after new people for God's kingdom. How was I to balance these two jobs? How was I to be a *servant* who took care of his congregation but also at the same time be a *leader* who spurred growth, *and* still have a life at the end of the day?

That's the essence of the challenge every leader faces if he leads people. Here's a quote not from the Bible but from the "bible of business," the *Harvard Business Review.* Their entire December 2001 issue was on the subject of leadership. In this issue, the *Review* compiled and reprinted many of their most-often requested articles on business leadership—the best of the best. One of the articles had this great insight about leadership and followers:

> Followers want comfort, stability, and solutions from their leaders, but that's babysitting. Real leaders ask hard questions and knock people out of their comfort zones and then manage the resulting distress.[4]

Now, this is not a quote from the Bible, but from *Harvard Business Review.* It's not written from a Christian perspective, but it does accurately express the tension every leader faces. Your followers—whoever they are, whether clients or customers, or employees within your organization—make three demands of the leader: comfort, stability, and solutions. That's what people want from you as a leader. They want you to solve their problems, comfort them, and provide stability. And there's nothing wrong with seeking to meet these three expectations. In fact, great servant-leaders work hard to provide all three. The leader who ignores these universal needs may soon discover he is out in front all alone, with no one behind him.

But if that's all you do, as the *Harvard Business Review* article says, you're babysitting and not leading. You may be a world-class servant, but a failure as a servant-leader because you have forgotten the mission side of leadership. As the article said, "Real leaders… knock people outside of their comfort zones and then manage the resulting distress."

It's when we try to be both servant- and growth-oriented that we find ourselves stretched. This dual focus requires the leader to balance the caring for the present with the pursuing of the future. Every leader has current customers, employees, and structures that need to be maintained and kept stable. But if all you do is care for the present, eventually you will die. To survive and grow, you must also have dreams for the future and go after new goals. And watch out, because if you focus on your visions at the expense of caring for your present people and circumstances, you'll end up with chaos on the home front. Both sides of the equation must be kept in balance. LESS IS MORE Leadership cannot remove this tension; it will always be there. Yet we will learn that a healthy balance *can* be achieved. You can maintain and pursue your mission and still have a life.

7. You Are a Limited Resource

As a leader, it is healthy for you to admit, "I am a limited resource." You have only a certain amount of time, energy, giftedness, resources, and money. You've got only so much to give, and when it's gone, it's gone.

As Christians, we have an *omni-everything God*. He can do it all. Nothing is too difficult for Him. By contrast, we are not omni-anything. In fact, we are *omni-nothing*. Compared to God, we are nothing. Now, it's true we have the power of God's Spirit living within us, and we have almighty God as our partner in our lives, but still, we are a limited resource. And as a limited resource, we need to have a method that will bring direction out of the madness we face as leaders. We may have all kinds of opportunities before us, but because of our limitations, we simply can't go after all of them. So how can we best spend the limited time, energy, and resources we have? *LESS IS MORE* will show you that leaders, as limited resources, must learn to simplify, reduce, and in fact "do less" in order to "accomplish more."

8. Leadership Is a Draining Experience

Leadership can at times be energizing, but it can also be draining. It involves giving yourself away, investing that "limited resource" in a cause, a mission, a business, a task. And when you give of yourself, you become drained. You go home at the end of the day and you do not feel as fresh as you felt when you left that morning. So not only are you a limited resource, but the demands of leadership can leave you exhausted.

When we look at the life of a typical pastor, it's easy to see why leadership can be draining. If a pastor wants to be a good ministry leader, he needs time to pray, study, be an ambassador to the community, and prepare his messages. He's got to be a loving shepherd of people. He's got to counsel people with problems. He's got to develop and maintain a model marriage if he's going to be any kind of an example. He's trying to raise a few healthy children for the same reason. He's got to do administration; the administrative demands can't be ignored. He's got to be able to plan and stay within a budget—not only at church, but at home, too. He's got to be a disciple-maker. He can't just win people; he needs to build them up in the faith. He's got to deal with the unexpected crises that are part of life in ministry. There's always a crisis going on somewhere in the congregation. And then he's got to be a worship planner. He's got to make sure worship happens

Pastor's duty—Jobs

well. He's got to have a vision and plan for the future. He's got to be a missions leader because the church must be concerned about the world. He's got to stay well-informed about the moral issues in our culture and lead his church in responding to today's moral decay. And then, at times, he's got to be the on-site "copy repairman" and find time to download the latest virus protection updates for the computer!

That's life for a pastor in the average church. And by the way, the average church has about 125 people and only one pastor, so yes, he does change the toner in the copy machine. Some churches are larger and have other pastors or staff people to help shoulder the burdens, but that doesn't mean life is any easier in a larger church. Remember,

Ministry Leader's Week...
Pray
Study
Community ambassador
Teach
Loving shepherd
Counsel
Model marriage
Administrate
Perfect family
Budget
Disciple maker
Crises
Worship planner
Vision
Mission leader
Champion of moral issues
Change the toner!

larger churches come with more people, more programs, more staff management, and more things to fix! The answer, as we will discover in our *LESS IS MORE* paradigm, is to simplify and focus so you can lead more and manage less.

When I began teaching these leadership principles to business leaders, a friend interrupted me and declared, "Well, Dale, that's your world, but I'm not a pastor or ministry leader. I'm in the real world." Perhaps you coach a team, lead a school, or run an office. Then let's look at your life, the Christian man or woman trying to lead and still live well.

First, you've got your job. This alone—with your commute time—usually takes a good 40, 50, or even 60-plus hours of your week. Then

Marketplace Leader...

Work
Study the Word
Prayer
Teach kids
Pray for kids
Correct kids
Time with spouse
Do budget
Fix broken stuff
Revise budget
Small group
Crises at work
Worship
Serve at church
Support missions
Confront moral issues
Download Windows patches!

on top of these demands, if you're a Christian, you need to study God's Word. You also need time to pray just to survive! You need time to communicate with God. If you're married, you best not forget time with your spouse. And if you're a parent, you need to be teaching your kids and be involved with their schools. You must also pray for your kids because you know that teaching them isn't going to fix everything. And when they don't obey you, you've got to take time to correct them and deal with their problems. Then there's your personal care, such as taking time to exercise and stay healthy.

You also have to keep track of your home budget and stay within the numbers because money doesn't grow on trees, and there's never quite enough. You've got to fix broken stuff, because if you own anything, especially a home, stuff breaks. I'm never quite sure if I own the stuff, or if the stuff owns me! There's always something that needs fixing, cleaning, or replacing. And home isn't the only place where crises arise. Problems crop up in the workplace, too. That means extra hours, often without extra pay. Then there's the mails—junk mail, email, and voicemail. They all demand some time and attention. The list is endless, isn't it?

You've also got to make sure you set aside time to go to church and worship. That's a priority. What's more, as part of the body of Christ, you ought to serve or help out somewhere. And you're also needed to help support missions and alleviate world hunger and confront moral issues in America. And for the sake of your spiritual growth, you want to be involved in a small-group Bible study.

And, as one businessperson cried out at one of my seminars, "And don't forget to download your software patches!" Patches and viruses are now a part of everyday life. No wonder we describe ourselves as busy, buried, and behind!

Does that describe your life? If so, no wonder you're tired as a leader. There's too much going on. Yet you could easily add another dozen tasks to my list above. All these little responsibilities are real and cannot be ignored. They add up quickly and fill up our lives until we cannot do one more thing.

9. More Is Not the Answer

Many of us believe more is the answer. We convince ourselves as leaders that the day we can grow a little *more*, make a little *more*, hire one *more* person, then our life will become *more* sane. Not so. I have never known growth to take away my sense of being overly busy and behind. Growth will, in fact, bring a new and *more* demanding set of problems. In all my years as a leader in churches that range from 28 members to over 5000, we have always needed one *more* assistant pastor and a few *more* thousand dollars. In every business, every busy leader feels a need for *more* resources.

> *Success and the growth that follows can actually make your situation worse unless you know how to manage it correctly.*

So what happens when you get a little *more* money or one *more* employee? With that new employee comes *more* what? Demands. Problems. Headaches. Management. You see, growth alone does not fix the leadership challenges you face—unless you know how to respond to those challenges in the midst of the growth.

Why does growth alone not automatically restore balance to the busy leader? Because growth produces more work. As my churches grew, every new member brought a new set of needs. Bigger budgets

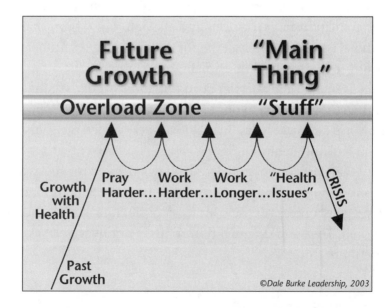

©Dale Burke Leadership, 2003

⟨⟨ ⟨ ⟩ ⟩⟩

The "Overload" Zone: A Typical Response

- Health leads to success.
- Success produces more "stuff."
- Stuff requires more management.
- The leader is distracted from his "main thing." The leader hits his or her overload zone.
- Growth slows or stops.
- Health issues develop.
- Lack of health leads to crises.
- Leader is further drained and distracted.
- Organizational decline or death soon follows.

The illustration maps the typical response I've observed over the years by Christian leaders who feel overloaded. Usually they respond by praying harder, working harder, and working longer hours. But this seldom restores the health of the leader or the organization. Eventually, if the leader does not adjust his method of leadership, health issues will put the church or organization into high-maintenance mode, then into crisis mode, and then into decline.

meant more money to be managed, spent, and tracked. Bigger congregations required more classes, more teachers, more ministry care.

What about the business leader? With every deal you close, there's a new relationship to maintain, a certain amount of follow-up that has to be done. With every product you sell comes a new customer to service. With every new step that you take toward your dreams you end up with *more* to do, not *less*. Success and the growth that follows can actually make your situation worse unless you know how to manage it correctly.

Our LESS IS MORE principles will offer you an alternate response to this invisible ceiling of "stuff." The answer is not *more*, but *less*. The leadership principles modeled by Jesus Christ and the early church always boost the power and potential of the leader while guarding his or her quality of life. Jesus valued both effective leadership and an abundant, joyful life. Every organization can grow without destroying the life of the leader.

The eight vital secrets of *LESS IS MORE Leadership* will enable you to *break through your "stuff," refocus on your "main things," and return to healthy growth with a balanced life*. That's the goal of our next eight chapters. You *can* lead and still have a life!

So far we've looked at nine facts of life for the twenty-first-century leader. And with each one, we've barely scratched the surface. With so much bearing down on us, it's no wonder we're feeling over-whelmed. But with the tenth and final fact of life for leaders comes some good news!

10. There Is Hope

My tenth fact of life for leaders allows us to end on a positive note: There *is* hope. Now why do I believe there's hope? Because I believe God desires for us to have healthy and growing ventures, whether in the ministry or the marketplace. Now, I'm not saying every business or church should expect dramatic growth all the time. Sometimes you're in a community or in a setting or circumstance that doesn't really allow for dramatic growth to take place. But I *am* saying God wants you and your organization to be healthy. Don't you think that's true?

The question is, how can we make that happen? That's what the next eight chapters are all about. I believe there is an approach to leadership that can multiply your leadership potential and, at the same time, protect your quality of life. Most of us have tried the *more* approach. Maybe it's time to try *less...less* of everyone else's demands on your life and *more* of God's grand design for leadership and life.

LESS IS MORE Leadership: An Overview

The eight principles we'll explore are all built on ancient yet thoroughly modern principles of leadership. They've survived the test of time, and they really deliver when put into practice. Each principle, when applied, will boost your leadership to a higher level.

⟨⟨⟨⟩⟩⟩

God Is the Owner, You Are the Steward

I believe, according to the parable of the stewards (see Matthew 25:14-29), that God wants you, the leader, to maximize whatever resources He has entrusted to you—for your benefit, for the good of the lives you influence and for the advancement of God's kingdom. You are a steward called to maximize whatever possessions, power, or leadership God has entrusted to you while on earth. Everything you own actually belongs to God. You are merely the temporary steward, or manager, of a part of God's creation. He created everything and owns it all.

God deserves excellence from you and your organization so that He might be glorified. This is true not only for His church but also for the life of every Christian leader. He wants every one of His leaders to be healthy and doing the very best job they can do leading whatever they are called to lead. There is no distinction made between the secular and sacred when we go to work. In both realms we are to lead well to the glory of God. The apostle Paul exhorts every Christian, as he goes to work, to serve as if he were working for his Lord (Ephesians 6:7). He then challenges every earthly master, leader, and business owner to remember that both employer and employee answer to the same Master in heaven (Ephesians 6:9). Every leader is a steward of all God has entrusted to him and is expected to maximize God's investment.

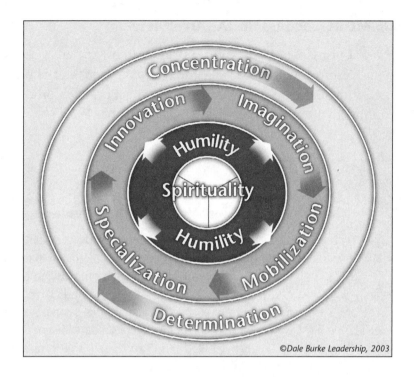

©Dale Burke Leadership, 2003

LESS IS MORE Leadership
Eight secrets for leading and still having a life!

Spirituality	*The Power of Convictions*
Humility	*The Power of Servant-leadership*
Imagination	*The Power of Vision*
Mobilization	*The Power of Letting Go*
Specialization	*The Power of Unique Abilities*
Innovation	*The Power of Creativity*
Concentration	*The Power of Focus*
Determination	*The Power of Hope*

It's also possible for us to define LESS IS MORE Leadership in a sentence:

LESS IS MORE Leadership
combines a Christ-centered philosophy of life
with a proactive, dynamic system for leadership
providing ongoing, lifetime guidance
for the pursuit of professional success
and personal satisfaction.

Let's break that down into parts:

Christ-centered philosophy of life—The LESS IS MORE approach is not me-centered but God-centered. It is built on the worldview that God exists, loves you deeply, and desires to be a part of your life and leadership. No matter what your job or ministry, ultimately, God is the One you serve.

Proactive—LESS IS MORE Leadership is not reactive but proactive, helping leaders regain control of what they do. It allows the leader to truly lead instead of follow, to act instead of react, to drive and not be driven by the pressures and demands of others.

Dynamic—The LESS IS MORE approach is not static but adaptive, changing with the leader and the challenges he or she faces. It also empowers, boosting leadership potential, enabling him or her to break through personal and professional barriers.

System—LESS IS MORE is not just about ideas but implementation. All eight principles are accompanied by specific action steps that will guide you beyond theory into practice.

Lifetime guidance—LESS IS MORE Leadership is not just a book of the month, but a philosophy for life. These eight universal truths are useful at every step of a leader's journey, and can propel any leader to higher levels of life and leadership. The principles speak to novices and veterans alike because the pursuit of excellence never ends for a leader.

Professional success and personal satisfaction—LESS IS MORE is not just about growth but also health. The eight principles will free you to pursue new goals and fresh dreams in your career, business, or ministry without sacrificing yourself or your family on the altar of success. You'll learn how to lead with vision and still have a life.

Therefore, *LESS IS MORE Leadership* is more than just a book filled with great-sounding quotes and ideas. These truths are not static but dynamic; you can return to them again and again as you map your future. They will provide you with new ways to think and act when you encounter today's challenges and tomorrow's opportunities. These truths, put into action, do not merely educate. They empower! They enable you as a leader and your organization to break through the overload zone and will enable you to begin to *really* lead...and love it!

The Inner Ring:
The Heart of the Leader

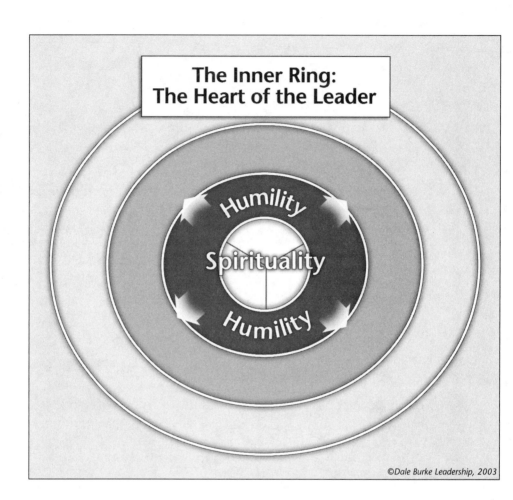

The Inner Ring:
The Heart of the Leader

Great organizations are built on great leadership. Great leadership requires great leaders. And great leaders are gleaned from the fields of good people—men and women of moral character, strength, and conviction. In today's world, there is a severe shortage of all of the above. So where should we begin if we hope to address the shortfall of great leaders? God's Book of Wisdom gives us our starting point:

> Watch over your *heart* with all diligence,
> for from it flow the springs of life (Proverbs 4:23).

Therefore, any wise approach to leadership must begin with the heart of the leader. Life is always lived from the inside out. So before we sharpen the skills of visionary leadership—Imagination, Mobilization, Specialization, and Innovation—or explore the components of effective execution—Concentration and Determination—we must go to the heart of the matter, the heart of the person called to lead.

First, **spirituality—*the power of convictions*** stabilizes the leader at the core of life, strengthening character and providing the moral guidance so necessary for great leadership in the twenty-first-century world we just discussed. We must be anchored in our faith and the wisdom of God. Spirituality is the hub of life and leadership. It answers the following:

Whose *voice* is most important

when everyone has a different opinion?

What *values* should never be abandoned

when others are willing to bend the rules or rewrite them?

Which *vision* is worth pursuing

when we can't do everything?

What are the *vital relationships*,

the people who really matter most?

LESS IS MORE spirituality seeks to simplify the life of the leader by focusing on fewer people to please, a few core values to protect, and a clear vision to pursue. Life is now coming into focus.

Second, **humility—*the power of servant-leadership*—**prepares the heart to go to work, to enter the middle ring of leadership with the right focus. If you want to be great, according to Jesus Christ, be a servant. Humility will indeed empower effective leadership in every segment of the middle ring. Humility calls us to serve God, our ultimate CEO, by serving others. It empowers and enhances every aspect of our lives and our leadership as we avoid the destructive temptations of pride, which always can be found lingering on the edges of our success. The "H Factor" of humility will enhance your leadership at every level. Humility, properly understood and applied, frees the leader...

- To more clearly see the future—the power of vision
- To more easily release management—the power of letting go
- To increasingly focus on areas of strength—the power of unique abilities

- To more quickly adapt and innovate—the power of creativity

What is humility—its essence and its expression? And where is the source if I need a fresh dose for my leadership? Leadership begins with these heart issues.

"No one can serve two masters;
for either he will hate the one and love the other,
or he will be devoted to one and despise the other."
—JESUS IN THE SERMON ON THE MOUNT (MATTHEW 6:24)

"Collect your thoughts, rally all your faculties, mass your energies,
focus your capacities. Turn all the springs of your soul into one channel,
causing it to flow onward in an undivided stream. Some men lack this
quality. They scatter themselves, and therefore fail."
—C.H. SPURGEON, GREAT NINETEENTH-CENTURY CHRISTIAN LEADER

"Resolve to perform what you ought;
perform without fail what you resolve."
—BENJAMIN FRANKLIN

"Let me tell you the secret that has led me to my goal:
my strength lies solely in my tenacity."
—LOUIS PASTEUR, GREAT FRENCH CHEMIST

"Ministry that costs nothing accomplishes nothing."
—JOHN HENRY JOWETT, EARLY TWENTIETH-CENTURY PREACHER

CHAPTER TWO

CHAPTER TWO

Spirituality—
The Power of Convictions

To be an effective leader, convictions are essential. Today's leader must know who he is and who he serves. For the Christian leader, the three V's of spirituality—the voice, vision, and values of God—serve to stabilize his soul and galvanize his character and conduct. The leader whose spiritual life is weak and ill-defined will find himself at the mercy of his world—a world that can never quite make up its mind what it wants. A world that cares not for the life of the leader, but only for what it can extract from him. It is a hungry world whose appetite is insatiable and whose demands can never be totally fulfilled. And if you want to avoid being a casualty of such a world, you need the type of strong convictions that comes from authentic spirituality at the core of your life.

Jesus said, "I came that you might have life, and have it abundantly" (John 10:10). It's possible, then, to be a leader and experience an abundant life. It must begin with your spirituality—your commitment to the *voice, vision,* and *values* of God. And the voice, vision, and values need to be lived out in the context of a fourth V, *vital relationships.*

As a Christian leader, your first priority in life is to answer these questions: Who's my ultimate boss, my final authority 24/7? If God is my Lord, then how and where do I connect with Him as the CEO of my life? How, in practical terms, do I bring Him into all I do as a leader?

Serving One Master

Does this mean God wants to micromanage your life? Not at all. God gives His children tremendous freedom and responsibility every day. He wants to "lead" your life, not manage it. But it's hard for that to happen if you're not looking to Him as your Master.

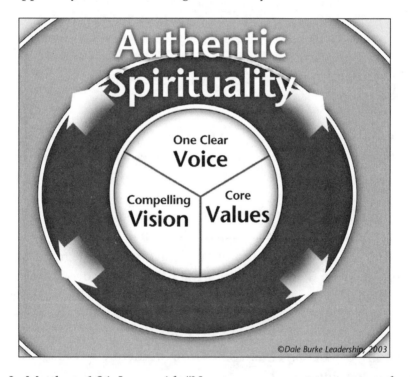

In Matthew 6:24, Jesus said, "No man can serve two masters; for... he will hate the one and love the other." It's impossible to serve two masters, and the two Jesus mentions here are God and mammon (money or wealth). Now, Jesus isn't saying there's anything wrong with possessing wealth. There's nothing wrong with making a living, and a good one at that. In fact, the parable of the stewards reinforces the value of doing the very best you can with your money, even multiplying it if you can. We just need to make sure God is our Master, and not the possessions He entrusts to us.

> *Because God owns your business or whatever else comes under your leadership, you're accountable to Him.*

So, who are you serving? Who is your boss? If you look to God as your Master—if you look to Him for guidance, wisdom, and direction— it should have an impact on every area of your leadership. In fact, spirituality can empower your leadership while balancing your life.

Now, you may be thinking, *Dale, that's easy for you to do. You're a pastor. You lead a church. A church is God's deal. It is the operation center for divine business on earth. So it's expected and natural for you to check in with God every once in awhile and ask Him what He wants you to do. But what about those of us in the business world?* Consider this: Whether you're in ministry or the marketplace, the principle is still the same: God owns it all. God is not only the God of the church, He's also the God of the universe. He's the creator of everything. As such, He owns it all. And we are stewards—not owners, but stewards of small slices of God's world. We are just temporary managers of His possessions.

If God owns everything on the planet, then ultimately He is the One whom all of us serve. The implications of that are huge: Because God owns your business or whatever else comes under your leadership, you're accountable to Him. It is vital you check in with Him because, after all, He is the CEO and all your service is to Him. Are you giving Him the final say as to how you live your life and handle the stewardship entrusted to you as a leader?

Now if God is the One you serve, then your relationship with Him deserves to be at the center of your leadership paradigm. Your relationship with Christ will bring not only conviction to your life as a leader, but you'll also end up simplifying your life. In today's fast-moving world, if you want to be able to run fast and adapt quickly, then you'll find conviction and simplicity a big help to you.

《《〉》》

Does the size of your ministry or business matter?

As we talk about the principles of great leadership, keep in mind that your measure as a leader has nothing to do with the size of your ministry or business. Consider that only one to two percent of the churches in America have congregations of more than 1000 people. God is not impressed or more pleased with me because the church I lead has over 5000 members. After all, it is His church, not mine. He built it, not me, and not even my predecessors.

God cares just as much about my leadership when I lead a church of 50, 150, or 500. God's goal is simply for me to be faithful. I need to do the very best I can do with whatever gifts and resources God has entrusted to my care. As long as I'm doing that, God will be pleased with me. Faithfulness is the goal, not size. In fact, the parable of the steward teaches that "he who is faithful in little will be faithful over much" (Matthew 25:21).

Just because God has permitted me to serve in a large church doesn't make me better than anyone else. I still need to be faithful to carry out my work diligently. I can't say, "Hey, now that I've reached this level, I can take it easy and just make sure I don't lose ground." I need to constantly ask, "God, what do You want me to do now? How can I multiply my impact for your kingdom?"

The bottom line is this: Are you being a good steward of what God has entrusted to you? That means everything—who you are as a person, your abilities, your mind, your relationships, and any opportunities or responsibilities given to you as a leader. Are you using all your resources to the maximum for God's glory? That's the true measure of a leader. Don't let the size of your organization discourage or inflate you. No matter what your size, and no matter what your business, keep looking for ways to increase your kingdom impact. You're being measured by your faithfulness.

Faithful & Fruitful!

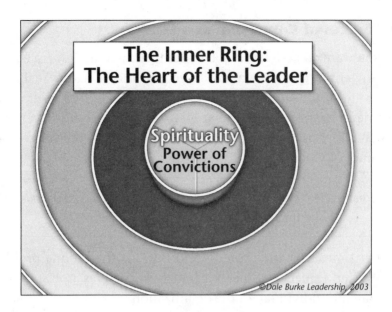

©Dale Burke Leadership, 2003

A Key Paradox

With that in mind, I want to introduce a paradox to you. Before I share it, however, I want you to consider a list of paradoxical statements. When I talk about the power of spirituality—these thoughts come to mind:

- In order to be relevant, stay *ancient.*
- In order to move *forward,* connect to the *past.*
- In order to *serve more* people, first *get away* from everyone.
- In order to *speed up,* first *slow down.*
- In order to *accomplish more,* go *take a break.*
- In order to *make a statement,* first *be quiet and listen.*
- In order to *get moving,* make sure you are *well anchored.*

If I were to summarize that list into one thought, it would be this:

> *The secret to being effective in the* **now**
> *is staying connected to what is* **eternal.**

The Sources of Conviction as a Leader

If you want to do a better job of competing in a high-paced, fast-changing environment as a leader, you need conviction at the core of your life. You need certainty. You need to anchor yourself in that which never changes so you can keep up with change and stay healthy. And that brings us to the first three V's of spirituality—the voice, vision, and values of God:

Great leadership is always based on the *voice, vision,* and *values* that transcend the *you, it,* and *now.*

What I mean by the "you, it, and now" is the unique profile of your life and leadership. *You* as a leader—indeed, as a person—are a one-of-a-kind individual. *It,* the organization you lead, is unique and different from all others. The *now,* the time in which you are living and leading, is unique in history. These three define you, your organization, and your environment. They are unique to you and nobody else on the planet.

As Christian leaders, we want the voice, vision, and values of God to be our first and most important touchpoint as we lead and live.

Responding to the "you, it, and now" is an important part of good leadership. But beware—when you operate in this urgent "response mode," you are at risk. It is dangerous to lead from the "you, it and now" until you are stabilized by conviction—that is, eternal and unchanging core values. Knowing who you are and whose you are as a child of God, should guide your choices in every arena of life. Knowing what should never change is the key to being able to respond to the times with healthy, innovative change. Knowing what is always true is the key to understanding the ever-changing now, which struggles to ever make up its mind!

As Christian leaders, we want the voice, vision, and values of God to be our first and most important touchpoint as we lead and live. They provide conviction at the core of our life and empower our leadership. They warn us when we are about to go too far, changing what should never change. They help us set and maintain priorities. They guide us in the tough choices and often simplify difficult decisions. They transcend the "you, it, and now." They transcend who *you* are as a person, they transcend the *it*, your organization or ministry, and they even transcend the *now*, the demands of your culture or times.

So that you have a better idea of what I'm talking about, let me give you an illustration. Let's say I've decided to begin a new church, and before I start, I go around and ask people, "What do you want from a church?" Then I use their answers to help me set up a church that matches what they want. There's no doubt that if I give people what they want, they will come and the church will most likely experience rapid growth. That's not a bad thing, but it's not the first or best thing to do. That's because I've let the "you, it, and now" dictate the very nature of this new church.

The better way to start a church is to first find out what God wants a church to be. No matter what the culture, no matter what the time period, no matter what the interests of the people I survey, and even no matter what my personal preference, I need to first be clear on what my Master and Lord wants the church to be. So rather than turn to contemporary culture, I need to go to the eternal principles of Scripture so that I hear God's voice, picture God's vision, and adopt God's values for this new church. Once I am anchored in His principles, then I can go to people and ask them, "What are you looking for in a church?" Then I can get creative and respond to their needs without compromising God's vision for the church.

This pattern applies to the business world as well. God's Word contains eternal principles on how to run any organization. God's voice, vision, and values will bring *conviction* to your life and leadership. Why is this important?

- *You need one clear voice* so that in times when you have conflicting opinions, you have an all-wise guide that is heard over all the other voices and directs even the toughest of decisions. I offer some practical suggestions for listening to the voice of God in this chapter. God loves you and those whom you lead, so expect Him to lead you as you listen. But don't expect Him to shout above the noise of your busy world. Learn to get quiet with Him, and with His Word, and listen. Later we will explore how to restructure your week to facilitate quality time with God in our seventh core principle, *concentration* (the power of focus).

- *You need clear core values.* These are your guidelines on *how you do business.* You base them on your convictions (which, in turn, are based on the truth of God's Word) and adhere to them regardless of whether they help or hurt you in the marketplace. These are the nonnegotiables of life.

- *You need a clear and compelling vision.* This vision is a portrait of where you, as a leader, are headed. And it's anchored in eternal principles that are just as true and relevant today as they were 100 years or 1000 years ago. This is your vision for your life and your leadership as you live to someday hear your Master say, "Well done, good and faithful servant."

And finally, these three elements need to be lived out in the context of the *vital relationships* in your life. Let's examine the first three V's, then see how they all connect to our vital relationships.

One Clear Voice

As a leader, you need to follow the voice of God. Seek to follow the Master's divine guidelines for who to be and what to do. This is an absolutely nonnegotiable element of your leadership. As we learned earlier, God is our ultimate boss, and you are best served by letting Him call the shots because...

- He loves you deeply
- His expectations are stretching but realistic
- His resources are sufficient
- He sees the big picture and the long-term view of your life

Let's look at each of these truths individually:

1. *God loves you deeply*. As Christians, we believe God the Father sent His only begotten Son to die for us on the cross. And we believe this great gift is the ultimate proof that God the Father has your best interests and His own glory in focus, no matter what He does in and through your life.

Romans 8:32 says that if God "did not spare his own Son, but gave Him up for us all—how will He not also, along with Him, graciously give us all things?" In other words, if God has already made the ultimate sacrifice for you and met your greatest need, then you can know He will take care of your other lesser yet legitimate needs in accord with what is best for your good and His glory. A seminary professor I knew years ago summed up this truth in this way: "If God gave His very best to meet your *greatest* need, surely you can now trust Him with all the *smaller* issues in your life."

2. *God's expectations are stretching but realistic*. God understands you as a leader. He understands your strengths, your weaknesses, your capacity. And He will stretch you—sometimes until it hurts, out of your comfort zone. But at the same time, God is realistic. He's not going to ask you to do something that will harm you, your family, or your personal walk with Him. Now, we can't always understand why He does what He does, but He is a realistic boss. He knows you better than you know yourself!

3. *God's resources are sufficient*. God's resources are not always sufficient by *our* definition. But God will give you what He needs to give you so that you can accomplish what He wants you to accomplish. He will provide whatever it takes for you to complete the task He wants you to do. After all, He's unlimited in His resources. He is omni-everything.

"There were many times, while leading the team building the international space station, when I wasn't sure how to meet the challenges we faced. The only thing I could do was to pray, cry out for help, and listen for God's answer."

—Vice president-deputy general manager at a major aerospace company

4. *God sees the big picture and the long-term view of your life.* No other boss can see your life the way He sees it. In fact, most bosses don't really care about the big picture and the long term. God does. He sees the impact of every decision on all those touched by that decision and its repercussions—the Big Picture. He sees how it will affect people you do not know and will never meet. He has a clear view of the long term and the eternal ramifications of everything—the ripple effect down through time and history!

Now how does this come into play in our lives? As leaders, we have to make decisions. We have to decide where to work, how to get that work done, which tasks to prioritize, and so on. For example, perhaps you've been in the position of having to decide whether or not to leave one job and go to another. As a pastor, I've been there—twice. The first time, I moved my family from Ohio to Pismo Beach, on the coast of central California. Seven years later we moved again—to Fullerton, California.

There were two big risks connected with the move to Fullerton. First, the pastor who preceded me had a national reputation, and he was one of my heroes, known for his exceptional teaching and writing. Pastor Chuck Swindoll had served the church for over 20 years and was deeply loved. The word on the street among my pastoral peers was not, "Who do you think will go to Fullerton?" Instead it was usually, "Who do you think will be foolish enough to go to Fullerton?"

The situation was often compared to the challenge faced by those who followed basketball coaching legend John Wooden at UCLA. Since Wooden's retirement, none of the coaches have survived for long. I realized that following Chuck Swindoll would not be easy. I could end up like those coaches who tried to follow Wooden, the legendary "Wizard of Westwood." In fact, in an open congregational meeting during the final interview process, a member (probably a UCLA alum) asked me if I was aware of this comparison, and if so, how did I feel about such a challenge? And I believe my response was a gift from God: "Well, I'm counting on two things. One, I'm counting on the fact that the members of this church are more gracious and forgiving

⟨⟨⟨⟩⟩⟩

Listening for God's Voice

Improve

- *Daily Time with God.* Develop the discipline of meeting with God daily. Open His Word and read, reflecting on its truths and principles. Read with a prayerful attitude, asking God to show you want you need to learn today. God often speaks when you are quiet and alone with Him in prayer and reading His Word.

- *Memorize His Word.* Find key verses in God's Word and commit them to memory. Meditate on them. If this sounds intimidating, simply start by writing key verses on life and leadership on small "business cards" and carry one in your pocket at all times. Read it several times a day. Before long, you will have it memorized. God often speaks to us by bringing His Word to mind as we make decisions.

- *Weekly Time in Worship.* Maintain a weekly time of worship. Don't just "go to church," but go with the expectation that God will remind you of who He is, what He has done for you, and the beauty of His love relationship with you as your heavenly Father. God often speaks as you focus on Him in worship.

- *A Group of Like-Minded Friends.* Meet regularly, either weekly or monthly, with a group of peers who share your faith and commitment to integrating God's values into every segment of life, especially your work. Ideally, find others who are in the same or similar occupations, or others who can help you process better the demands you face every day as a leader. God often speaks through friends who also have a relationship with Him.

- *Monthly Refocus Time.* Some leaders find it helpful to set aside a half a day each month, or even a full day, to be alone and review life. Pray as you reflect on your priorities and review your key objectives. Then ask God to guide you as you adjust for the coming month. God often speaks when you slow down and review what matters most.

- *Annual Retreats.* At least once a year, get away for a few days of rest, reflection, and relaxation with God. Use this time to reevaluate and refocus your life and leadership. Read God's Word and just think about your life. Ask God to bring to mind ideas for refining your priorities or plans. God often often speaks when we get away from the noise of everyday life and think, alone, with Him.

than the UCLA alumni. [And I've found that to be true!] And second, I'm counting on the fact that I believe God wants me to do this. And if God is in it, I trust I'll be okay."

> It is safer to be out on a limb with God than to sit in a rocking chair at the base of the tree without Him.

The second risk connected with the move to Fullerton was the fact my family would have to be uprooted and relocate with me. I knew my wife, Becky, was committed and that she would love me through the move even though it took her away from her friends. But Becky and I worried most about how our kids would respond to the idea of moving. We figured it didn't make sense to ask the kids about the move ahead of time, because we knew they would vote against it. Instead, we went to God and asked Him what He wanted us to do, because He is our Master. And if He told us to move, we trusted God would help our kids survive such a monumental change in their lives.

After it was clear that God was opening the door, we broke the news to our kids in a restaurant booth while on a trip. I will never forget that day. They were shocked. Then they began to cry. After a short time, our son began to warm to the idea. Our younger daughter then added, "I guess it'll be kind of a neat place to live. We'll be closer to some cool stuff like Disneyland." Our oldest daughter, however, jumped up and ran out of the restaurant in a fit of grief and anger. Begrudgingly, she made the move with us. But several months later, on Father's Day, she wrote me a card and said, "Dad, *thank you* for making me move. It's the *best thing* that ever happened to me in my life." Later she met a young, sharp assistant youth pastor named Josh, and fell in love. And now life is sweet and good for Mrs. Beth (Burke) Rose—all because we made her move to Fullerton.

When it came to making a decision about these risks, I went to God. Why? Because as I said earlier, He cares about us, and only He can see the big picture of our lives. As leaders, it's much better to put our decisions in His hands than keep them in ours. Put another way, it is safer to be out on a limb with God than to sit in a rocking chair at the base of the tree without Him. That's true in connection with every leadership decision we make, whether in a ministry or a business.

So as you try to lead and balance all the demands on your life and make hard choices about your priorities, why not consult with the Boss? Let Him lead in your life. His loving leadership will bring conviction, security, and wisdom to the very core of your life and your leadership.

Remember, God sees both the *global* and the *eternal* consequences of every decision you make. That's a staggering thought, isn't it? We see only the immediate consequences, which is why we sometimes don't understand why God allows certain things to happen. We say, "God, You blew it." But the reality is, God looks way beyond the immediacy of our pleasure or pain and sees the global and eternal ripple effects of everything that happens. And He is wisely guiding us for our good and His glory.

Uncompromised Core Values

The second component of authentic spirituality is your *core values*. These core values are the Master's eternal guidelines on how to do business—not *what* to do, but *how* to do it. These core values are convictions you will not abandon even if they threaten your success. In the book *Built to Last,* which was a secular bestselling book on leadership, authors Jim Collins and Jerry Porras did a detailed study of what they called long-term visionary, enduring companies.[1] These companies ranked at the top, the best of the best statistically, over a period of more than 50 years. Their earnings exceeded the Dow Jones averages and the other stock indexes that Collins used to measure them against other good businesses. They were not just good companies, but great ones. They were enduring, they were visionary, and they had successfully survived transitions from one leader to another.

One quality Collins noticed in every one of these companies was that they had strong core values. Collins defined their core value with the following definition:

Something that you will not abandon even if it hurts you in the marketplace.[2]

I like that definition. Whether you lead a church or a corporation, you need core values that you will hold to even if they slow you down or take you out of business. It is these values that will help protect you whenever you face the temptation to compromise. Your core values provide convictions that keep you stable as a leader—principles you will not bend on.

⟨⟨⟨⟩⟩⟩

Core Values of the Fullerton Church

At the church I pastor in Fullerton, we use the acronym B. GREAT to remind us of values we want to uphold in all we do in our ministry:

B is for *biblical*. We want to keep God's Word as our final authority for all we do and believe.

G is for *grace*. We want to teach grace and be gracious.

R is for *relevance*. We want to be in touch with the culture and the "real world" of our congregation and our community.

E is for *excellence*. We want to do everything with excellence, because God deserves our very best.

A is for *authenticity*, both in our person and practice. We want to be real and authentic in all we do.

T reminds us we want to do ministry in *teams* that *trust* each other and work *together*.

What are some core values you can develop as a leader to guide you in your business or ministry? When you create your core values, keep them short and memorable, and then test your life and leadership against them as you implement them.

A Compelling Vision *For your Life—At the Finish Line*

The third element of an authentic spiritual life is what I call a *compelling vision*. By this I don't mean strategic plans and ideas for the future of your company. Rather, I'm talking about the big picture of your life. I'm not concerned with what you hope to be next year, or even five years from now. I'm talking about you at the finish line of life—you remade into the man or woman God wants you to be.

Compelling Vision:
The divine portrait of me, the servant-leader,
transformed into the person the Master wants me to be.

So, I'm not talking about what you see in the mirror today, but about a clear picture of what kind of person and leader God wants you to become. This compelling vision will birth new convictions that will direct you as you set your course to not only "do something" but "become someone." Without this clear picture of what God wants you to be, has designed you to be, and redeemed you to become, you will forever be confused and confounded by life's choices. I cannot promise you that you'll become all you dream of becoming as a leader. But if you don't even have "the dream," I can assure you that you'll never even come close.

Do you have a picture in your mind as to what good, godly *leadership* looks like? And what a good, godly *leader* looks like? An exercise you may find very helpful is to get a piece of paper and ask God to help you write a description of what kind of leader you want to be 10 or 20 years from now. Get as specific as possible and see if you end up with some great goals you can work toward, both in your personal life and in your ministry or business. In case you're wondering what this list could look like, here's my "compelling vision." Feel free to let it get you started!

> «‹›»
> "Two of life's most important journey questions are 'Who am I?' and 'What am I trying to accomplish with my life?'"[3]
>
> —JOHN BRADLEY
> AND JAY CARTY

Authentic spirituality can empower your life, strengthen your convictions, and stabilize your leadership. Less is more. Simply follow one *clear voice* (God as Master), adhere to *core values* (on how to do work or ministry), and possess a *compelling vision* (know what we want to become). Now the heart of the leader is focused on what really matters. One of those is our fourth V—the *vital relationships* of our lives.

《《〈〉》》

My Compelling Vision

At my memorial service someday, I hope my associates, friends, and family say, and actually believe, the following:

- He loved His Lord and served Him faithfully to the end.

- He loved his wife, Becky, and cared for her, cherished her, and helped her become all that God created her to be. He helped her blossom!

- He nurtured and loved his three children (and possibly grandchildren), and saw them all come to personal faith in Christ and begin their own journey toward maturity. He did all he could to live as their hero and role model.

- He was a faithful steward of all the resources God entrusted to him, investing his time, money, and abilities for maximum kingdom value.

- He pastored his church with integrity and a commitment to the Word of God, always teaching and leading with excellence.

- He was a lifelong learner, always pursuing Christlikeness and making progress until he died.

- He loved people more than his personal pleasures and was willing to flex to serve the needs of others.

- He achieved to the best of his God-given abilities yet stayed humble, always giving the glory to God for whatever was accomplished in his life.

- He enjoyed life and rejoiced his way through its ups and downs.

Paying Attention to Vital Relationships

As we listen to God's voice, follow His values, and pursue His vision for life and leadership, we must remember the second half of the great commandment. The first, as Jesus said, is to love God with a passion (Matthew 22:37-38). That's what we've been talking about: following His voice, living by His values, and pursuing His vision. This great commandment continues, "And love your neighbor as yourself" (Matthew 22:39). These two components to great leadership should never be neglected—the centrality of your relationship with God, and the importance of your relationships with people. When you strengthen your relationship with God and your relationships with family, friends, and others around you, you'll lead and still have a life.

©Dale Burke Leadership, 2003

Have you ever noticed how, after a serious tragedy such as a tornado, earthquake, or hurricane, we'll hear people stand together with their family members and say, "At least we have each other"? There's no question relationships are important. So we must guard them and make them the best they can be. We must fight to never let the pressures of leadership cause us to compromise time with our kids, spouse, or friends. Don't place business or ministry ahead of people. After all, at the heart of every great ministry or business we find people. Every business is a people business. And the people who matter most, in the long run, are the ones we come home to at the end of the day. Loving is indeed at the center of all leading, and all of life. My first book, published in 1999, was a book on love. *A Love That Never Fails*[4] is a study of love as defined by 1 Corinthians 13, a great passage on love. In the end, my ability to love is my greatest tool as a leader. Show me a truly great lover of people, and I'll show you a success story every time!

> ⟨⟨⟨⟩⟩⟩
>
> "As Chief of Staff at a major hospital, and director of all emergency services, I learned years ago to 'hire nice.' I look for young doctors who know how to be nice to people, to communicate care and concern. I can teach them all the medical skills they need, but I can't teach them 'nice.'"
>
> —DR. DAVID REED, WEST ANAHEIM MEDICAL CENTER

Are you listening to God's voice? Following His values? Seeking His vision of you at the finish line? When you do, you'll know authentic spirituality, cultivate conviction, and experience the benefits that come from keeping your focus on one master—*the* Master. That's all part of loving God. And loving people is a part of listening to His voice. It's not merely optional, but a necessary core value. And loving people helps you to better shape your vision for the future...making you a better leader. But above all, live and lead to please God—not the members, not the customers, not even your family—just God. The rest will fall into place.

LESS IS MORE Leadership:
Putting *Spirituality—the Power of Convictions* into Action

1. *Hear His voice*—God is one great boss; listen to His **voice** and follow Him.

   When and where do I plan to nurture my spiritual life?

   (Review the sidebar "Listening for God's Voice" on page 61.

2. *Practice His values*—God provides eternal guidelines, our core **values** for life.

   List and review your core values, which should never change even if they hurt you, your ministry, or your business:

3. *Pursue His vision*—Summarize, in a paragraph, your **vision** for your life as a leader:

   What do you want to be said of you at your memorial service? And what needs to change to move you toward that kind of reputation?

"Whoever wishes to become great among you shall be your servant."
—JESUS TO HIS KEY LEADERS (MATTHEW 20:26)

*"We were surprised, shocked really, to discover the type of leadership
required for turning a good company into a great one....
good-to-great leaders....are a paradoxical blend
of personal humility and professional will."¹*
—JIM COLLINS, AUTHOR OF *GOOD TO GREAT*

"Servant leadership propels organization success."²
—KEN BLANCHARD, EXPERT BUSINESS CONSULTANT

"A great man shows his greatness by the way he treats little men."
—THOMAS CARLYLE, NINETEENTH-CENTURY SCOTTISH HISTORIAN AND WRITER

"Pride goes before destruction, and a haughty spirit before stumbling."
PROVERBS 16:18

"No grace is stronger than humility."
—RICHARD SIBBES, SEVENTEENTH-CENTURY MINISTER

CHAPTER THREE

Humility—
The Power of
Servant-leadership

———

When Jesus trained His disciples, He knew He was training them for a monumental work that would span the globe. He knew they needed to not just be good leaders, but great ones. At the same time, He knew the danger that a prideful spirit could pose to the health of the movement He was about to birth. Such pride, inflated by success and so commonly found among leaders, could undermine the success of this new venture. So Jesus shocked His disciples with a new leadership model, the servant-leader.

It should not surprise us that Jesus would call the Twelve to be servants. In fact, Jesus Himself said He had come to serve, not be served (Mark 10:45). The surprise is that Jesus said whoever wanted to be a great leader needed to be a servant. Serving others in humility does not lower one's leadership potential, it actually increases it! Less "me" in my leadership makes me *more* of a leader. Less is more!

Humility—A Desired Trait

That God values humility highly is revealed in 1 Peter 5:6, which warns that God is "opposed to the proud, but gives grace to the humble." First Corinthians 13:4, when describing the nature of love, declares, "love...is not arrogant." And James 4:10 says, "Humble yourselves in the presence of the Lord, and He will exalt you." Humility is indeed the path to greatness in your life and leadership.

Humility expresses itself through the practice of serving others. Humility asks God, the Master, "What do You want me to do?" The answer: "Think, act, live, and lead as a servant."

The Inner Ring: The Heart of the Leader

Humility

Spirituality

Power of Servant-leadership

©Dale Burke Leadership, 2003

Humility Does Not Weaken, It Empowers

Humility and serving others are often associated with weakness, surrendering control, or being someone else's "slave." No wonder it has little appeal in today's world! Serving, then, is viewed as being for followers and not leaders, for the weak and not the strong. Humility is expected from employees, but seldom from the employer, and certainly not from the person at the top—the one who calls all the shots. Yet Jesus, the greatest leader who ever lived, was proud (appropriately, of course) to choose the role of servant and called others to follow His example with humility.

At times, Jesus' leaders-in-training became prideful—and it showed in their arrogance and their "jockeying" for positions of power. But after Jesus' death, they remembered His example and His messages on humility. They finally understood, and this changed their leadership and their lives. They came to realize that servant leadership is key to

Servanthood in no way lessens you as a leader. In fact, it empowers you, increasing your leadership potential.

leading and living well. The apostle Paul, the ultimate CEO of the early church, declared in Philippians 2:3-5:

> Do nothing from selfishness or empty conceit,
> but with humility of mind
> regard one another as more important than yourselves;
> do not merely look out for your own personal interests,
> but also for the interests of others.
> Have this attitude in yourselves which was also in Christ Jesus.

Notice that Jesus willingly took on the role of a servant in spite of the fact that He "existed in the form of God" (Philippians 2:6). Jesus was no wimp or weakling. He was a strong leader who knew how to get things done. In fact, He was God incarnate! He was so strong He was omnipotent. Yet at the same time, He was the supreme model of humility and servanthood.

Based on Jesus' example as a great leader, we can forever put to rest the idea that servanthood equals *inferiority*. Or that humility is a sign of *weakness*. Servanthood does not mean *passivity* and just doing whatever people want you to do. Jesus was always in control, making His own choices, doing what He wanted to do. In fact, He lived out His mission in life perfectly. He was infinitely gifted and powerful. *He was omni-everything!* He was God in human flesh. And yet He took on the role of a servant as He led. So servanthood in no way lessens you as a leader. In fact, it empowers you, increasing your leadership potential. Less is more. Focusing less on yourself makes you a more potent leader. Humility is at the core of great leadership.

Humility a Key Trait in Great Leaders

I love it whenever secular research affirms biblical truth. One place I saw this evident was in Jim Collins's bestseller *Good to Great*. This book, along with *Built to Last* (which was coauthored with Jerry Porras), is the result of extensive professional research on the nature of great companies and the great leaders behind them. When Collins studied these "good to great" leaders—the best of the best—he discovered several common traits shared by them. He wrote:

> We were surprised, shocked really, to discover the type of leadership required for turning a good company into a great one. Compared to high-profile leaders with big personalities who make headlines and become celebrities, the good-to-great leaders seem to have come from Mars. Self-effacing, quiet, reserved, even shy—these leaders are a paradoxical blend of personal humility and professional will. They are more like Lincoln and Socrates than Patton or Caesar.[3]

Jesus Christ was yet another great leader with both drive and humility. In His leadership, He demonstrated both key attributes: personal humility and professional will.

In his book, Collins uses a metaphor that I believe is worth gold to any leader humble enough to apply it consistently. It goes like this: A great leader, in *good times*, goes to *the window*, and in *bad times*, goes to *the mirror*. In good times he goes to the window and looks out at the parking lot and he sees the cars, the employees, his team, and declares, "Wow, what a blessed leader I am to have these people working here! What a great job they've done. I'm so fortunate to serve alongside such gifted people."

In bad times he goes to the mirror on the wall, looks at himself, and reflects, "Where did I go wrong? What did I miss? Why didn't I see this coming? Shouldn't I have at least anticipated this and tried to head it off?" He takes responsibility.

Collins then studied a set of corporate leaders who were good but not great by his statistical profile. Again, these were not losers. They were winners, in the short run. But they never achieved the status of a "good to great" leader. One consistent pattern was how they responded to their successes and failures. They reversed the window and mirror. In good times, they went to the mirror and said, "Look at me. What a great job I am doing! The team is sure lucky to have me at the controls." And in bad times, they went to the window and exclaimed, "Who messed up? Who should I fire or replace? Someone is to blame, and I want to know who!"

The point is this: In good times, great leaders go to the window and share the success with the team. They recognize that it's not just about them. In bad times, great leaders go to the mirror and take responsibility before casting blame on others. They own the problem, even if they didn't directly cause it. Lesser leaders reverse the order. In good times, they go to the mirror with pride. And in bad times they head straight for the window to cast blame.

Now let's apply this window-and-mirror metaphor to our lives. If you're a pastor, you spend a lot of time working hard on sermons. Perhaps your listeners don't fall asleep on you, but neither do they seem to be energized by your messages. Do you go to the window or the mirror? Do you go to the window and say, "I wish my people were more teachable, more responsive, more willing to obey God and do what I tell them to do. They just don't care. They just don't get it."

Or do you go to the mirror and say, "Whoa, that message didn't seem to connect. What could I have done to teach that truth more effectively?" Do you take a look at your own sermon development and look for ways to change, improve yourself, or be more creative or clear as you communicate?

Here's another illustration: It's time to recruit more helpers for the children's ministry classes as the school year starts. Every church goes through this, right? You put together a recruiting campaign. You create a video presentation of the children's ministry program, come up with a theme, and distribute letters, flyers, and posters. You promote the need for helpers and make pleas from up front. Then when it's time to launch, some of the classes still don't have enough teachers. Do you go to the window or the mirror?

If your tendency is to say, "People today just won't serve like they used to," you're going to the window. But is the problem the people, or the leader and his leadership? Maybe you need to go to the mirror and ask, "How else could I have done this?" Maybe you haven't sufficiently communicated the vision, or the value of changing the heart of one child. Maybe you or your fellow leaders need to rethink how to approach recruiting. Maybe you need to restructure the program or change the job descriptions.

Volunteers

〈〈〈〉〉〉

The Benefits of Humility and Taking Risks

First Evangelical Free in Fullerton may be a megachurch, but we are just like every other church when it comes to recruiting volunteers. It doesn't matter the size of the church; we've always been shorthanded when it comes to recruiting helpers, especially for the children's classes. The first Sunday of October is promotion Sunday, during which the kids in each grade move up to the next grade level. In my first seven years at the church, we had several classes that could not open because they weren't sufficiently staffed. It would take several more weeks of hard work and recruiting before we finally had all the classes staffed. It just seemed that people weren't willing to serve like they used to!

In 2003 we decided that in order to expand our outreach to the community, we needed to change from two services in the morning to three. Now this, of course, completely upset the paradigm at our church. It meant shorter services and shorter sermons. It meant reshuffling all the adult classes, changing the setup for our parking lots, and reallocating many of our staff. And it also meant spreading our children's ministry out over three services instead of two. You can imagine how everyone responded, then, to the idea of adding a third service!

At first a lot of people said this just couldn't be done. The Sunday schedule had been the same for 22 years, and the changes required to add a new service were just too great. But we plunged forward, and when we went to the three-service format, for the first time in my years in Fullerton, every children's class was fully staffed and open—with some volunteers in reserve! Why?

In humility, we transformed our approach to better serve the needs of our potential volunteers. Under the new three-service schedule, a person could now volunteer to teach children and not have to stay at church for nearly three hours. Originally our morning was broken into two longer blocks of time, starting at 8:50 A.M. and ending about 12:15. Our two services were an hour and 15 minutes in length. Between those two blocks was a 45-minute break to allow for turnaround time in the parking lots.

In order to provide three services in the morning and open up a 50-percent growth potential per week, we had to take a risk and rethink our entire approach. "What if we did a one-hour service? Could Pastor Dale reduce his sermons from 40 minutes to 30 without giving up our core value of quality biblical teaching?" I gave it a try, and guess what? They've become some of my better sermons. The shorter time has made me a better teacher. Our worship services are crisper and even leave people wanting a little more. That's not a bad thing at all. And the biggest surprise of all? Our children's ministries were 100 percent staffed!

Apparently our old schedule had worked against us, and we didn't even know it. But because it had been in place for 22 years, no one questioned it and thus, we were shooting ourselves in the foot. Once we were willing to look in the mirror and come up with a new vision, and with humility, change our approach, good things began to happen.

As a leader, when problems arise, you need to have the humility to ask yourself, "What did I *contribute* to this?" Or, "How could I have *prevented* this from happening?" Don't look for someone else to blame. You will empower your leadership when you practice humility and encourage your leadership team to do the same.

Humility and Pride—a Comparison

Before we can benefit from the power of humility in our leadership, we need to know what humility looks like and what it does. We can also get a clearer picture of the nature of humility by contrasting it with pride. Here is the power of humility in a nutshell.

What Humility Does

Humility accepts responsibility. That's the point of Jim Collins's metaphor of the window and the mirror. A humble leader examines himself before he looks to others as the possible contributor to a problem.

Humility promotes objectivity. The humble leader sees reality more clearly, is open to honest feedback, and doesn't react against the "bearer of bad news." He realizes that, in reality, there is no bad news if it is truth. Truth is always your ally, never your enemy, so seek it and accept it.

Humility increases teachability. A humble leader listens to and learns from other people, whereas the prideful leader thinks he knows it all. When the leader's ego is wrapped up in his service, his product, or whatever his claim to fame, he will be less open to needed change.

Humility stimulates creativity. A humble leader thinks out of the box and innovates. This leader has a "we always can do a better job" attitude, and his eyes and ears are always on the alert for new ideas.

> *People are drawn toward and stick like glue to humble leaders.*

Humility expands flexibility because the humble leader adapts more readily. Teachability and creativity foster flexibility in both the leader and whatever he or she is leading. Any church or organization that wants to stay in business for the long haul needs to be willing to flex with circumstances and people. If the world is changing and you don't, you'll soon be left behind.

Humility boosts team morale because the humble leader recognizes and appreciates others. Prideful leaders tend to take way too much credit for their successes. Humble leaders are quick and eager to pass the praise and appreciation on to others in the organization or ministry. Such praise takes team morale to new heights!

Humility fosters loyalty among your staff members, both paid and volunteer. People are drawn toward and stick like glue to humble leaders, which results in long-term relationships. They flee prideful leaders and are repelled by their arrogance and self-centeredness.

Humility pursues excellence. A humble leader acknowledges there is always more to learn. I recently read a quote from one of history's greatest hitters in baseball, Tony Gwynn. Tony was the first player since Stan Musial to win three consecutive batting championships. And Tony

<<<>>>

"If I have done my hiring correctly, I have competent associates who can challenge me and make us all better if I don't let pride get in the way. I have tried to allow my associates to use their organizational and analytical gifts to create templates and library comments for fairly complex appraisal reports. As a result we have some terrific spreadsheets and other tools that we wouldn't have if I tried to remain in complete control of all those aspects."

—Commercial real estate assessor

once said, "I really don't think I'll ever be satisfied. Once you think you're where you want to be, you're not there anymore."[4]

As a leader, you should always strive to develop and grow. We can easily become the victims of our own success. One of the first steps toward failure is always success. In any leadership challenge, success can set you up for failure. That's because success tends to produce pride, and pride then produces complacency: "We're the best; we've got it figured out; you should see the way we do (whatever)." And as soon as that prideful attitude settles in, you stop pursuing excellence because you're convinced you have arrived!

Ancient scripture addresses the very real danger of pride and offers an alternative. In Philippians chapter 3, the apostle Paul gives some great leadership advice:

> I do not regard myself as having laid hold of it yet...
> But this one thing I do: forgetting what lies behind
> and reaching forward to what lies ahead,
> I press on toward the goal for the prize
> of the upward call of God in Christ Jesus (verses 13-14).

His "one thing" was the constant pursuit of excellence. It takes humility to forget the past. Past successes can foster pride, and past failures can foster frustration. Instead of looking back at your successes and failures, focus forward, always humbly seeking to grow and discover a better way.

Humility brings balance. Why? Because the humble leader trusts others and can share the burden of leadership with his team. The person who is prideful needs to micromanage, stay in control at all times, and make sure they get the credit. They just can't let go. But the humble leader can go home and relax, and leave the office or ministry in the hands of a teammate. Why? It's not about themselves.

Humility promotes and maintains relevance. The humble leader, with a servant's mindset, focuses continually on the needs of others. When you take the role of a servant, whether in a business or a ministry, you will keep asking the people you serve:

Member Survey

"How's it going?"
"How am I serving you?"
"What's working and what's not?"
"Any suggestions?"
"What do you need from us?"
"What do you want from our ministry/business?"
"What do you expect as a member/customer?"
"What problems can we help you resolve?"

The message you want to send as a church or a business is, "I'm here to *serve* you, not *use* you. I'm not here to plug you into my programs. I'm here to develop programs that serve your needs. I am your servant." When you maintain that attitude, your church or organization will always stay on the cutting edge of relevance. And you'll remain innovative, creative, and responsive because you're orientating yourself to your consumers. That's great servant leadership.

Jesus was right when He said, "If you want to be great, be a servant." I've had business owners tell me, "In my business, when I start thinking that the customer is lucky to have me, I begin to lose out to the competition. To stay on the edge, I need to constantly listen to the customers, find out what they're thinking, discover their needs, and even anticipate the need that is just around the corner, even before they encounter it. When they finally see it, I'm there eager and ready to serve them. That's cutting-edge relevance. But if I'm still selling a product, or a service, that no longer fits their needs, I'll soon be going out of business." In other words, they realize pride will put them on the road to irrelevance. Here's why…

What Pride Does

In a leader, pride is costly and destructive. It is the inverse of humility:

- Instead of taking responsibility, you *blame others*. Surely someone else is at fault if things are not working out.

- Instead of being objective, you live in *denial*. The prideful leader of a church or a business will choose to ignore what is obvious to

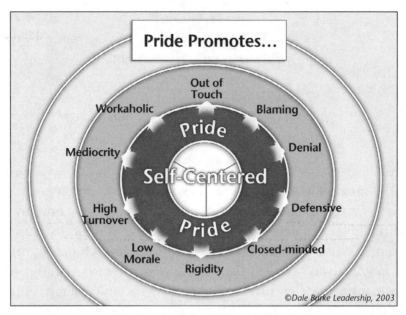

©Dale Burke Leadership, 2003

everyone else. If something isn't working, you just turn the other way.

- Instead of being open-minded and receptive, you are *close-minded* or *defensive*. The prideful leader guards the "sacred cows" of the church, the business, and says, "This is the way we've always done it."

- Instead of flexibility you have *rigidity*. "We do it my way or I'm out of here." The ghosts of the past, especially past successes, will haunt you and hold you back.

- Instead of team spirit, you end up with *low morale*. The prideful leader inflates himself and deflates others. He always wants to take credit for the successes. His best staff or volunteers eventually get discouraged and leave for a better place to serve.

- Instead of loyalty, you experience *a high turnover rate* among the volunteers and paid staff. If you want to keep your people, serve them and watch for ways to help them become more productive workers. Help them succeed, and give them the credit.

- Instead of excellence, pride sees itself as great, but actually ends up *settling for mediocrity*. When you are driven for your own profit, and not the profit of those you serve, your members, staff, customers, productivity, and innovation will soon spiral downward.

• Instead of balance, you end up becoming a *workaholic*. Because of pride, you find yourself wanting to be in control. You have to do it all, hold the reins tight, stay in control.

• Instead of being connected, you find yourself *out of touch* with the client, the customer, the church member, or the community you're trying to reach. Pride causes you to think it's all about you when really it's all about them.

Philippians 2:3-4 couldn't put it any clearer: "Regard one another as more important than yourselves; do not merely look out for your own personal interests, but also for the interests of others." Take on the role of a servant, like Jesus did. Humility is at the heart of good leadership.

Five Important Phrases: How to Speak "Humility"

The power of humility is unleashed in your attitude, your actions, and even in your language. Learn to speak with humility. Start by learning and rehearsing the five most basic phrases in the language of servanthood. In my LESS IS MORE Leadership seminars, I've had leaders tell me this simple list helped their leadership more than anything else. These five phrases will enhance your leadership vocabulary and empower those around you. Unfortunately, they are often missing or underused by leaders in both the ministry and the marketplace.

Hello
Please
Thank you
Can I help?
I'm sorry

As leaders, we need to get very comfortable with these five phrases. When spoken from a humble heart, they will flow easily and often,

《《〉》》

Purpose Beyond Profit—
to Be Great, Be a Servant

Note the servant mindset of a dozen of the most successful and enduring corporations. The following statements are excerpts from their mission statements as found in the book *Built to Last* (by Jim Collins and Jerry Porras, pages 68-71). Note what is emphasized:

3M: "Our real business is solving problems."

American Express: "Heroic customer service."

Ford: "People as the source of our strength."

General Electric: "Improving the quality of life."

Hewlett Packard: "We exist as a corporation to make a contribution."

IBM: "Making customers happy."

Johnson & Johnson: "The company exists to alleviate pain and disease."

The Marriott: "Friendly service and excellent value...people are #1."

Merck: "We are in the business of preserving and improving human life."

Nordstrom: "Service to the customer above all else."

Wal-Mart: "We exist to provide value to our customers."

Walt Disney: "To bring happiness to millions."

It really *is* all about others. To be great, be a servant!

and they will communicate to people that you truly value them. There is indeed some truth to the idea that everything you need to know in life you learned in kindergarten!

Hello: "You are noticed"

One of the ways you can express humility is by simply saying hi, hello to those you encounter. That may seem a small thing, but it means so much to others because it communicates that you value them. I've tried to make this a way of life. It's hard because our church is large, but I still try my very best to connect with as many people as possible and say good morning, or hello. I stop and ask them about their kids, or better yet, engage the kids in conversation, preferably down at "kid eye-level." Show a sincere interest in people, acknowledge their presence, and they will feel loved and valued. When you take the time to do this, you'll stop people in their tracks. And they will be drawn to you as a leader. So take time to greet people and acknowledge them from a genuinely humble heart.

Please: "You too are busy, and I value your help"

Saying *please*, instead of just giving orders, communicates that you respect others and that you see them as equals and not subordinates. It lets them know you value their time and appreciate their willingness to put your needs on their agenda.

Thank you: "You are appreciated and not taken for granted"

Saying *thank you* to people who serve alongside you (I don't like the phrase "under you") communicates that you value their contribution and help. Even if they are paid to do a job, simple and frequent words of appreciation endear the team members to their leader. Every one of us loves to be noticed for what we do, great or small, to move the mission forward. Saying thank you, even to your customers, lets them know you really appreciate their time or business. I try to thank every new attendee who comes to our church. They didn't have to come, and I want them to know I'm honored they gave me some of their valuable time!

Can I help?: "I'm here to serve with you; we're in this together"

Offering to help demonstrates that the leader is willing to serve as well as be served. Every leader, on occasion, needs to model the role of a humble servant. He needs to get down and dirty, to jump in the trenches with the troops. The "leader as helper" will seldom lack the appreciation and loyalty of the team.

Now, I'm not saying leaders should simply do anything that needs to get done. God wants leaders utilizing their unique abilities and devoting the majority of their effort and energy to whatever is of greatest strategic importance to the business or ministry. Yet, as the Lord leads, you should be available to serve with a no-job-is-beneath-me attitude. Just as Jesus washed the feet of His disciples, great leaders know how and when to humble themselves and serve the team.

I'm sorry: "I make mistakes too; please forgive me"

Can you remember the last time you said, "I'm sorry, please forgive me" to a member of your team? To a client or customer? To an assistant or secretary? If you can't, you may be struggling with pride. Why? Because none of us are *that* good. I know I'm not. And by God's grace, I do the best I can as a leader. But sometimes I still don't get it done when I said I'd have it done, or I still show up late when I should have been there on time. I still do a task at a lower level of excellence than I know I'm capable of. And I still forget or become clueless when I should have remembered. All of us fall short at times. It's human nature on this side of heaven.

Now maybe you seldom miss the mark. Maybe you're more together than I am. But none of us is perfect. We all make mistakes. And when we do, we need, in humility, to be quick to say, "I'm sorry." People will love you for it and it will empower your leadership.

Ways to Cultivate Humility

Now that we've seen the power of humility, we're ready for the really hard question: How can we cultivate this important attitude? I had to wrestle with that when I wrote my book *A Love That Never*

Fails. The book is a study of 1 Corinthians 13, in which the apostle Paul lists the qualities of true, godlike love. One of those qualities is that "love...is not arrogant" (verse 4). The fact that arrogance is the opposite of humility got me thinking. So what is it that nurtures humility and insulates us from pride? I came up with a list of several ways to nurture humility; here are my top five:

Study God, the Omni-everything
Face Yourself, the Omni-nothing
Study the Fruit of the Spirit
Listen to Honest Feedback
Focus on Grace

Study God, the Omni-everything

At the top of the list is *study God*. Study His person and character, and fall in love with Him. The more we focus on who He is and understand Him, the more we will realize our lack and where we need to grow. We are spiritual creations, made in His image. When we become Christians, we are reborn that we might grow to more and more reflect His image. Yet every time we get a glimpse into God's character, we should realize how far we have to go to truly be like our heavenly Father. That is enough to keep us humble.

Face Yourself, the Omni-nothing

Another way you can nurture humility is to put a little plaque on your desk that says *I'm an omni-nothing*. Refresh yourself with that thought every day. You are a limited resource. You cannot do it all. You are not the center of the universe. When you remember that it's God who is at the center and that He is omni-everything, you'll feel humbled.

Study the Fruit of the Spirit

Review the fruit of the Spirit, God's description of what His Spirit should produce in your life: "love, joy, peace, patience, kindness, goodness, faithfulness, gentleness, self-control" (Galatians 5:22-23). As you realize how often these traits may be lacking in your life, it's humbling. Memorize or meditate on this list frequently, and you'll be reminded of the growth that still needs to take place in your life.

Listen to Honest Feedback

Listening to others helps bring *accountability* to your life. Allow those who know you best the opportunity to be honest with you. This is not about soliciting your enemies to beat you up, but asking your friends to build you up, with honesty. Honest feedback helps you see your weak points so you can do something about them. Humility is a valuable by-product of an honest look in the mirror. And friends and family, if asked, usually provide the clearest reflection!

Focus on Grace

The final, and perhaps my favorite way, to cultivate humility is to *focus on grace*. The more you study grace, the more you will be humbled. I guarantee it. The Christian concept of grace is best understood by comparing and contrasting it with two common terms: justice and mercy.

Justice IS giving someone *what they deserve*.
Mercy is NOT giving someone *what they deserve*.
Grace IS giving someone *what they do NOT deserve*.

Justice is not a bad thing. God is just, and at times in business or in relationships, it is appropriate to seek justice. Mercy is not bad, either. It is an act of kindness to withhold from someone the punishment they deserve. Grace, however, is the ultimate act of kindness and love. Grace not only withholds punishment (that's mercy). Grace adds blessings—gifts that are totally undeserved and unearned by the recipient.

Christianity is unique among all world religions with its emphasis on grace. Jesus provided, through His death and resurrection, forgiveness and life for those who would simply trust Him, receive Him, place faith in Him as their Savior and Lord. As Ephesians 2:8-9 says,

$\langle\langle\langle\rangle\rangle\rangle$

Where's the Fizz?

While I have delivered sermons for a good number of years, I still like to have someone critique my messages on occasion. I've had lay leaders, fellow staff members, and even student interns fill out sermon evaluations. Their feedback has taught me more than you can imagine!

I'm sure you've heard the expression, "Kids say the darndest things." Well, I believe a leader's most honest feedback usually comes from his or her own children. When my kids were younger, I would ask them, "Hey, how was the sermon today?" "Oh, I liked it, Dad." "Well what did you like about it?" "Well, you know, what I really liked was..." and they would give it to me straight. None of this polite, back-of-the-church sweet talk I'd often get from members. Interestingly, people simply wouldn't mention the hard work I had done analyzing a biblical passage. Rather, they usually pointed to an illustration or a story that brought the whole lesson together and made it applicable to them.

Well, one day I was riding home with my son, who was about nine or ten at the time. For some reason I sensed that the message that morning hadn't gotten people's attention in the usual way. So I asked him, "What did you think of today's sermon?" I'll never forget his response: "Dad, you're *usually* pretty good." And then he paused. I knew this was *not* going to be good. Then he laid it out: "Today's sermon was kind of like soda pop that's been sitting out too long. The soda is still there, but there's just no fizz."

I have never forgotten that comment from my nine-year-old "preaching professor." From that day on, every time I'm putting a wrap on a sermon, I now ask myself, "Where's the fizz?" What is it in this message that's going to speak not just to people's heads, but their hearts? How can I communicate this truth or illustrate this principle so it grabs their attention? That's what I now call the fizz factor. That day, my young son not only humbled me, he taught me.

So, whether you're in business or ministry, you may want to ask your spouse or kids to critique your work. Find someone who can give you honest feedback, and be willing to listen. They may very well say something that increases your "fizz factor" and keeps you from going flat!

"By grace you have been saved through faith; and that not of your-selves, it is the gift of God; not as a result of works, so that no one may boast."

Our very relationship with God is a gift, not something we earned. It was an act of mercy and grace. What a humbling thought! Religion itself can actually be a source of pride, if one believes they have gotten their act together and impressed God with their good deeds, acts of kind-ness, or religious piety. Christianity, however, has no place for such pride because it is not about *our* good works, but *His* good work—the work of the cross. It has nothing to do with our self-righteousness, but the righteousness of Jesus Christ, our Savior. No one earns the right to be a child of God; it is a gift to those who will receive it by trusting in Christ.

> *However high we've climbed…we've been supported by a "ladder of grace."*

Now, how does such grace promote personal humility in the heart of the leader? A Christian leader may be tempted to separate his sal-vation by grace from his occupation, which entails work. "Haven't I still worked to build my church, to build my business, to become suc-cessful as a leader?" No doubt, every leader has needed to show up, put out the effort, and work for what he or she has achieved. What's more, Scripture esteems hard work. Yet as Christian leaders we are who we are merely by the grace of God. By grace we were saved through faith. By grace we received new life in Christ. By grace we were set free to live the life we now live. By grace we are free to create as chil-dren of the Creator. All our gifts and abilities are "grace gifts" (see Ephesians 4:7), meaning they were gifts from God, not something earned.

Therefore all our achievements are ultimately gifts of God's grace. However high we've climbed in our profession, we've been supported by a "ladder of grace." Yes, we've had to work hard and seek to excel. But if it were not for the "ladder," even our best efforts would have been futile. We have no reason to be prideful over anything that we accomplish. God gets the credit, not us.

Summary Page

On to the Middle Ring of Leadership

This completes our look at the inner ring of leadership—the heart of the leadership process. We explored the heart of a leader, prepared and empowered by...

Spirituality—*the power of conviction.* This stabilizes us with the moral guidance we need to encounter the challenges of our world.

> We know whose **voice** is most important ✓
> when everyone has a different opinion.
> We know what **values** will not be compromised
> when others are willing to bend the rules or rewrite them.
> We know which **vision** is worth pursuing
> when we can't do everything.
> And we guard those **vital relationships**,
> knowing it's people who really matter most.

Less-is-more spirituality leaves us with fewer people to please, a few core values to protect, and a clear vision to pursue. We now know what really matters. Less is more at the core of our life means less urgency and more peace, less confusion and more clarity, less dissatisfaction, and more contentment. Our spirituality, our faith, and the convictions that flow from them now begin to stabilize our leadership and our lives. This doesn't remove the tough challenges we will face daily, but it does stabilize us for the battle.

Humility—*the power of servant-leadership.* If you want to be great, according to Jesus Christ, be a servant. Humility shifts our focus outward, on others and off of ourselves. Humility calls us to serve God, our ultimate CEO, by serving others. It empowers and enhances every aspect of our lives and our leadership as we avoid the destructive temptations of pride, which tend to flow from success. Humility builds up and brings together the team, while pride tears down and repels those around you. Humility will enhance your leadership at every level.

Now we're ready to bring the four V's—voice, values, vision, and vital relationships—into the middle ring as we move our mission forward. And we need to bring our humility as we move on to the middle ring, where we will learn how to envision the future, set goals, mobilize new leaders, and innovate with creativity. It all starts with *spirituality* and **humility**. Once those are in place, you are now ready to move on to the middle ring of leadership:

Imagination—*The Power of Vision*
Mobilization—*The Power of Letting Go*
Specialization—*The Power of Unique Abilities*
Innovation—*The Power of Creativity*

Let's move on and learn more about great leadership—the less-is-more kind!

LESS IS MORE Leadership:
Putting *Humility—the Power of Servant-leadership* into Action

1. What do you plan to do this year to esteem, honor, and encourage your team for their strengths and/or successes?

2. Is there an area of your business or ministry that is struggling and in which you need to take the initiative to solve the problem or make improvements? Explain.

3. Which of the five phrases of humility (hello, thank you, please, can I help?, and I'm sorry) do you need to use more often, and why?

4. Where are you most susceptible to pride and its negative effects on your leadership?

5. Pick one of the "Ways to Cultivate Humility" (see pages 83-88) and try it, asking God to increase your personal "H-Factor."

The Middle Ring:
The Heart of Leadership

The Middle Ring:
The Heart of Leadership

Innovation
Imagination
Humility
Spirituality
Humility
Specialization
Mobilization

©Dale Burke Leadership, 2003

The Middle Ring:
The Heart of Leadership

Great leadership with a balanced life always begins in the heart of the leader—the inner ring of leadership—which is comprised of spirituality and humility. Spirituality provides the power of stabilizing convictions—vision and values that will not be compromised. Humility produces a servant attitude, a focus on meeting the needs of others. Yet we have all known spiritual, humble people who can't seem to get anything done. They make great friends, but disappoint as leaders. Great leaders know how to move the mission forward.

Now we're ready to move on to the heart of the leadership process, to the four disciplines in the middle ring. Together they make things happen. They advance the mission. These four disciplines are absolutely essential for becoming a great leader and taking your business or ministry to the next level and beyond:

The Middle Ring—the Four Disciplines

Imagination unleashes *the power of vision.* Every organization needs a dream, a future, a hope of what could be. The leader paints a portrait of this envisioned future for all to see. This vision motivates and moves the team to tackle new goals that will advance their mission.

Mobilization lightens the load on the leader and empowers the leader as he or she releases aspects of the mission to other managers and leaders. I call this *the power of letting go*—the "lead more, manage less" principle. The new goals of your vision cannot be accomplished without mobilizing new leaders. The leader can now expand, lead, and still have a life!

Specialization taps *the power of unique abilities*, helping you to focus on the areas in which you are most gifted, and to lead from your strengths. As the leader lets go of whatever is outside his or her area of unique abilities and releases leadership responsibilities to his or her team, he or she is able to focus on *less* to accomplish *more*. This is the key to increased effectiveness and enjoyment in leadership.

Innovation relates to *the power of creativity*. This is the "What If!" principle, which keeps you moving forward with creativity as a leader. Without innovation, every church or business faces the same future— death from irrelevance. As creativity energizes the mission with fresh ideas, new dreams are imagined, vision is stimulated, and the cycle of organizational life rolls on!

Why These Four Essential Disciplines?

All four disciplines are essential to great leadership. Drop any one of them, and you will soon be in trouble. Imagination and vision, without mobilization (the power of letting go), will wear out the leader as he spreads himself too thin as a limited resource. Mobilization is fostered by fresh imagination and vision. Followers need to know where they are headed, and why they are going there. Only then will they sign on, pay the price, and invest their valuable time to make it happen. If you have mobilization without specialization, you'll find yourself aimless and underutilized, and perhaps even bored. And even the best imagination, mobilization, and specialization—in an ever-changing world—soon becomes ineffective or irrelevant without an infusion of creativity and innovation.

Note also in the diagram that all four disciplines are intimately connected to the inner ring of spirituality and humility. The Christian leader must continually maintain his heart, his love for God, and his desire to please the one Master as he envisions new goals and pursues new dreams. He must continually nurture humility and a servant spirit if he wants to be effective in every discipline found in the middle ring. So as we explore imagination, mobilization, specialization, and innovation, don't leave spirituality and humility behind!

Portrait of the Future

where headed?

+

why go there?

*"We need to learn to set our course by the stars,
not by the lights of every passing ship."*

—OMAR NELSON BRADLEY,
GENERAL AND FIRST CHAIRMAN OF THE JOINT CHIEFS OF STAFF

*"Make no little plans. They have no magic to stir men's blood
and probably themselves will not be realized.
Make big plans. Aim high in hope and work."*

—DANIEL H. BURNHAM, FAMOUS ARCHITECT WITH
INFLUENCE IN DESIGN OF MODERN SKYSCRAPERS

*"You shall be my witnesses, both in Jerusalem,
and in all Judea and Samaria,
and even to the remotest part of the earth."*

—JESUS, FINAL LEADERSHIP ADDRESS (ACTS 1:8)

*"I do not regard myself as having laid hold of it yet;
but one thing I do: forgetting what lies behind
and reaching forward to what lies ahead,
I press on...."*

—APOSTLE PAUL, EARLY CHURCH LEADER (PHILIPPIANS 3:13-14)

"I have a dream."

—MARTIN LUTHER KING

CHAPTER FOUR

Imagination—
The Power of Vision

Go back with me to the time of settlers and pioneers, of wagon trains filled with pioneers eager to go west with a dream of reaching the blue waters of the Pacific. As the western frontier opened up, these pioneers gathered in cities like Chicago and St. Louis with a common vision to go live in the beautiful new land called California. They signed on together to make the journey. They would load up their possessions in wagons and set out on what, in those days, was a long and dangerous trek. But they had a dream of a new and better life, so they put it all on the line, and started the adventure of a lifetime.

These people did fine at first as they crossed the western borders of Illinois and Missouri. But when they crossed the Great Plains, the going got rougher. They had to work to survive. Then they would cross into eastern Colorado and, upon approaching the region now known as Colorado Springs or Denver, they would see the jagged peaks on the western horizon get bigger and bigger. The next thing they knew, they were staring up at the Rocky Mountains, a massive barrier between them and their dream. They had never seen mountains like these before. The mountains they had known were more like hills, small indeed by comparison.

Even in the summer, snow could be seen on some of those Rocky Mountain peaks. That night, around the campfire, some began to have their doubts. "Whoa. Are we taking this wagon, our family, our kids, and all we own over this terrain? Is California worth it?" Others began to look around at this eastern slope of the Rockies and think to themselves, *You know, this is a pretty nice place right here. There's plenty of fresh water flowing year-round out of the snowmelt from the mountains. There's plenty of game. It's nice, flat land. It would be easy to build on this land, and others are settling here. Why not just stop, stay here, and settle down?* Then someone spoke, "Why would anyone want to cross those mountains? We've already come so far. Besides, isn't this place good enough? Yeah, it's *good enough* for me." I call this the Colorado Syndrome—"It's good enough; let's just settle down."

Friend, *good enough* is the death of most businesses and churches. Every business and church starts as a pioneer venture. But as time passes, we come face to face with the pioneer/settler tension. The temptation to settle for less and let go of the dream can be great. Our inclination, especially when facing a challenge, is to declare, "This is good enough" and just settle. *Another pioneer bites the dust and the settlement has added one more settler to its population.* How do you keep your team pushing forward toward the goal?

The way to overcome this Colorado Syndrome is to cast a clear and compelling vision of the future. When the travelers said, "This is good enough," they needed a leader to remind them, "Yes, this looks good here, but wait till you get to California! There's great land for farming, the mountains and the ocean are right next to each other, and the land is really cheap. And eventually, Hollywood, Disneyland, Malibu Beach, and the ski resorts of Big Bear and Mount Baldy will all be in your backyard! You can surf in the morning and be on the ski slopes in the afternoon. You can't do that in Colorado. And your farm will someday be worth enough to buy your own town in Colorado!" (Well, maybe the trail boss wouldn't have envisioned quite all those details. Forgive me, but I am from Southern California!)

Once the travelers are reminded of the benefits of continuing on to California, they'll receive a fresh burst of motivation. People need a clear picture of where they are going so that they can realize that it's worth the pain and the sacrifice to keep reaching for the goal. In your workplace or church, beware of the danger of telling people where you want them to go without reminding them of what they will gain when they get there. If you want to keep your team members from saying, "This is good enough," help them imagine the future. You as a leader must keep the vision fresh, alive, and always before them.

Becoming a Visionary Leader

In their book *If It Ain't Broke...Break It!*, Robert Kriegel and Louis Patler wrote, "Goals have their place...following dreams. They do serve a purpose. They give us something specific to shoot at...a way of keeping score. But if goals are to be beneficial...they must be guided by something larger and more encompassing, something that inspires us and infuses us with passion, creativity, and courage."[1]

Jesus knew the power of vision. He modeled this in His final declaration to His leadership team before He ascended to heaven. This declaration is known as the Great Commission. In it, Jesus did more than simply set out a goal; He gave His disciples a dream larger than any of them could imagine on their own. He told this small group of pioneer-leaders, "You will take this movement to the entire world."

Jesus had already taught them the first priority, loving God—that's spirituality. He had modeled for them the second priority, serving people—a heart of humility. Now,

> *Faith always focuses beyond the present, beyond "what is" to "what could be."*

before leaving them to direct the "company" from headquarters (heaven), He challenged them not to forget the mission—the very purpose behind the creation of the company! As we learned earlier, one of the hidden dangers of servant-leadership is that your preoccupation with serving your present members or customers can become the number-one obstacle to reaching your future members or customers. Success always produces "stuff," and this "debris of success" can distract you, drain you, and deny you from moving forward with the mission.

The Great Commission models for us the "Imagine This" principle. Jesus told His disciples, in essence, "Imagine this!" when He painted for them a vision of their future: "This is where you're headed. Go for it! You're going to start in Jerusalem, spread into Judea and Samaria, and then move onward to the outermost parts of the world. Every nation is going to know about Me and receive My message."

Now in A.D. 33, when Jesus made this proclamation, the nations didn't know about Him or His movement. And the disciples did not have a clue about how they were going to accomplish this. But Jesus painted a picture of where they were headed and challenged them to go for it. That's what I mean by the power of vision—helping people imagine, by faith, what could be that "is not," and what could happen that "has not." Faith always focuses beyond the present, beyond "what is" to "what could be." As Scripture says,

> Faith is the assurance of things hoped for,
> the conviction of things not seen....
> without faith, it is impossible
> to please [God] (Hebrews 11:1,6).

As you lead in the workplace or ministry, you must provide others with a vision of what kind of company or ministry you want to be— what kind of service you want to offer, what sort of product you want to produce. Not until your followers get a glimpse of the "future us" will they know where they are headed and what they must do to get there.

The Questions That Help Shape a Vision

Now, when you present a vision, there are at least three questions you need to be ready to answer:

- **The Destination Question**   *Where are we going?*
- **The Roadmap Question**   *How do we plan to get there?*
- **The Value vs. Cost Question**   *Why bother?*

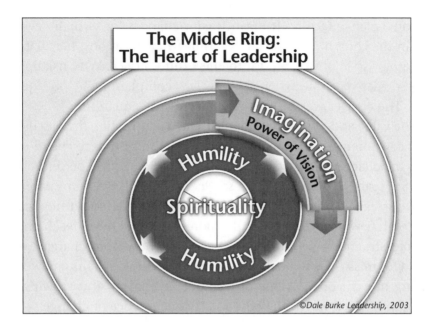

©Dale Burke Leadership, 2003

First, the destination question: Where are we going? If we do this, where will we end up? What's the goal or result? Better yet, what is the dream? If you want people to cross a mountain range, you must describe for them the life that awaits them on the other side of the mountain.

Second, the roadmap question: How do we plan to get there? Can we do this? People need to know there *is* a pass over and through the mountains. They must have a sense of hope that the destination is indeed within reach and not a dead-end canyon. In short, the trail boss must assure them that he has a plan, a way to get them over the mountains.

Third, the value-versus-cost question: What is the cost of making the trip, and why is it worth it? What value is there in making the hard journey over the mountain, especially if we are comfortable right where we are?

Our church's recent change from two services to three is a great example of determining the value versus cost. The plan called for a total restructuring of the morning schedule we had followed for 22 years! The cost in dollars was minimal, but the real cost was the "inconvenience factor." It meant major changes for virtually everyone in the church. It involved new times, new locations, new habits, and a new style of worship for the new third service. Why risk upsetting so many people when no one was complaining? Good question. The answer was in the value side of the equation.

The value added was tremendous: The new structure increased our ministry potential by 50 percent without requiring us to spend millions of dollars enlarging our buildings. We would add 50 percent more parking space by adding a third service. We would open up space for new classes and ministries. All of which meant we could now connect with new men, women, and children we could never reach under the old structure—people whose lives have now been changed forever. Our mission is to reach people. So the cost was definitely worth paying in light of the value of new people coming and growing in their faith—well worth the cost and inconvenience of change.

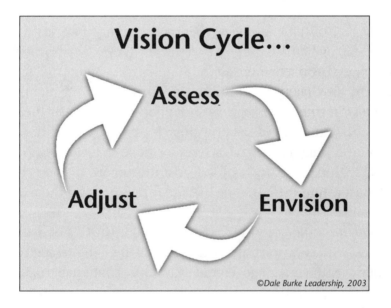

Vision Cycle...
Assess
Envision
Adjust

©Dale Burke Leadership, 2003

The Steps to Shaping a Vision

Now, developing a new vision or goal doesn't just happen automatically. There's a three-step process that will help you to cast a fresh vision, and get it moving without overloading yourself or your team. Remember, the goal is not only visionary leadership, but healthy leaders. The three key words here are *assess, envision,* and *adjust.*

Assessing the Past

First, assess your past. Ask the question, How are we *really* doing? with the emphasis on the word *really*. Sometimes this is not easy to do. We can be our own worst enemy when we look back and see only our good results and fail to consider signs that point to a need for change.

For example, during World War II, Winston Churchill was frustrated because he sensed he was not getting the unfiltered, full truth from the front lines of the war. So he developed a separate office that bypassed all the administrative layers of the military and government that would dilute the information before it got to him. This office allowed him to get war data that was more accurate and, as a result, Churchill was in a much better position to lead with wisdom.

You see, people don't like to deliver bad news to leaders whom they love. People also avoid dropping the "hard truth" to leaders whom they fear. Few people are willing to risk making the boss mad. This is especially true if the leader is your pastor. He's the one who may have officiated your marriage, dedicated your children, or sat with you in the hospital. He may someday speak at your memorial service! Nobody likes giving pastors bad news.

You may find this true in your organization or ministry as well. If people don't like something you're doing, or if they see a problem, they often hesitate to tell you the hard truth. Yet the hardest truth of all is that we really need to know reality if we hope to lead well. Bad news may be hard to face, but ignoring it doesn't mean it isn't out there. Tough truth is patient. It will not go away. It will eventually find itself into the light of day.

How can you work around this tendency of followers? Do what Churchill did. Set up some simple systems by which you can gather objective truth from the front lines so you know what is really going on. Find out from your members or customers what they truly think about your product. Ask the kids in the youth ministry what they think about their class or youth events. Don't just go to your managers and directors. Ask the end users.

Assessing Yourself and Your Team

Recently I asked the leadership board and pastoral staff at our church in Fullerton to do a one-page critique on me. I wanted to know two things: 1) How is my teaching and preaching ministry? and 2) How is my leadership? This wasn't a big or complicated multipage survey. My experience tells me that such long surveys may look impressive, but they seldom get processed or utilized. When you do assessments, create simple feedback forms. Ask about four or five questions, and give them to several people who serve under your leadership and to some people whom you are accountable to in your work or ministry.

You can also use the same surveys to solicit feedback from those who serve under other leaders in your church or workplace. The key is to create an atmosphere in which such feedback is a regular part of the pursuit of excellence by everyone in the organization (see the seven tips on page 110).

On a survey or assessment form, I always ask for more good feedback than bad. That's one of the principles that helps make this more constructive. I always ask for three or four points of encouragement but only one or two concerns, criticisms, or suggestions. You can do this in regard to both your work and your character. Ask for input on your character—your two or three strongest attributes. Then ask for one suggestion for your personal growth as a follower of Christ.

A lot of people at my LESS IS MORE Leadership seminars say, "My goodness, I can't even imagine what people would say about me." But there's no reason to be afraid. Don't be afraid to discover the truth. Just because you aren't aware of the truth doesn't mean it's not out there. People have opinions, and until you find out what they are, you're going to lead in darkness because you don't have the facts. Try my simple survey and get the truth!

Here's a sample survey:

⟨⟨⟨⟩⟩⟩
How Am I Really Doing?

It is my desire to grow as a leader, and I cannot do it without your feedback. Please take a moment to fill out this form. Please be gentle, but honest and specific. Then return it by mail to _____ by _____ . Thanks so much for serving with me and being a part of the team!

1. What do you appreciate most about my work or area of ministry?

 What are its strengths? List three or four items.

2. What one or two aspects of my work or ministry need improvement? Where are we weak? List one or two items.

3. What are my *personal strengths* as a leader? In relation to my character, conduct, or style, what do you appreciate most? List three or four items.

4. Where would you suggest I focus as I seek to grow and improve as a leader?

List one or two items.

5. On a scale of 1 - 2 - 3 - 4 - 5 - 6 - 7 - 8 - 9 - 10
               (Help!   Weak   Average   Strong   Super!)

How would you rate my work/ministry this year?
Now _____ One year ago _____

How would you rate my personal leadership and character?
Now _____ One year ago _____

For additional comments or feedback, use the back of this form.

⟨⟨⟨⟩⟩⟩

How am I really doing?

"Truth is always the ally,
never the enemy, of good leadership."

I was slow to understand the value of honest feedback as a young leader. Today, I realize that truth is an essential first step in my pursuit of excellence. It is good for me, for the church, and for our relationship. While leaders may find the truth painful at times, it can also help and heal. The key is the way it's delivered.

First, make it routine, not responsive. Assess your staff and their ministries regularly as a part of the ongoing pursuit of excellence. This prevents the more hurtful assessments done only in response to problems.

Second, lead with the positive. Ask for three or four things you appreciate most about "John or Jill Smith" and his or her leadership. Get feedback on that person's strengths.

Third, solicit specific suggestions. Tell your respondents, "Please be gentle, but honest and specific." Ask them for one or two suggestions for improvement. "How can I better serve you as a leader? What one or two ideas do you have for the organization?"

Fourth, listen "up and down" the organizational structure. Listen to both mature lay leaders below you and the supervisor or the board above you. Sometimes the view is quite different from below than it is from above!

Fifth, do a prayerful self-evaluation. Fill out a sheet on yourself. Ask God to show you your strengths and weaknesses. Ask, "How am I *really* doing?"

Sixth, set new goals. Set a course for growth next year that allows for your vision balanced with the wisdom of trusted advisors.

Finally, set new priorities and protections. The board should make sure the leader is "off-loading" before "reloading." Permission is given to *not* do certain things, in order to invest more energy and resources into new initiatives. Make sure your leader has a plan for protecting his personal and family life.

Assessing the Mission

You, the leader, must describe your vision and help your team see the value of going for it.

Not only do you need to assess yourself and your team, but you also need to take an honest look at your mission and ask, "Are we getting the job done?" Assessing your mission, including each vital component of your purpose or vision statement, is the best first step toward setting new goals. An honest look "in the mirror" is always the place to start in strategic planning.

For example, I often take our church staff and/or leadership board out of town on a weekend retreat for assessment. During our time together, we talk about each major aspect of our church's mission statement (which, by the way, comes right out of Scripture). We start by discussing our worship. We ask each other, "What are the strengths of our worship? Let's come up with a list. What's really working well?" During assessment, it is always important for you to identify your strengths so you can protect them and build on them.

Then we ask, "What's not working so well? What needs to change or even be terminated?" After we finish our discussion and spend some time in prayer, we ask, "Based on this information, let's set one or two goals for our worship this next year." Then we move on and discuss the other areas of our mission statement.

You can carry out a similar process at your business, organization, or ministry. The key is to do an honest assessment of each key area, determine the strengths and weaknesses, then come up with one or more goals to go after as a team. It all begins with an honest reality check: "How are we *really* doing?"

Envisioning the Future

After you *assess* the past, then you can *envision* the future. You can ask, "What are our dreams? Where do we want to go, and why?" Keep in mind the tendency of all followers to settle down, like the pioneers at the beginning of this chapter who were struck by Colorado Syndrome and became "good enough" settlers.

You, the leader, must describe your vision and help your team see the value of going for it. Show them that the work necessary to reach the goal is indeed worth the cost. When you do, they will become motivated. But if you don't stimulate their imagination with your vision, they will slow down and then settle, saying, "This is good enough." Here's why:

Settlers without vision
will always choose comfort over inconvenience.

If you don't want to settle for your present situation, lead with vision. And be aware that it will take work to stimulate and motivate your team to keep on pioneering, to keep on stretching. We all tend to prefer the comforts of the settlement over the rigors of the trail. We tend to choose the grocery store over the garden, or fast food over cooking up a meal ourselves. Why? It is easier. But when we *assess, envision,* and *adjust,* we set ourselves up to break through the overload zone and reach new goals.

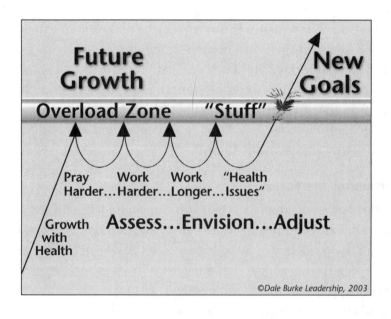

"I took the board of directors at Willow Creek to some inner-city ministries that we're funding and providing volunteer help for. We were in an empty warehouse; it must have been 95 degrees. The humidity was incredible. But the person leading this ministry stood and said, 'Imagine that corner of this warehouse filled with electrical supplies. A skilled worker from a church could stop here, pick up all the supplies he or she needs, then go over to the home of someone in need and fix the wiring.

"'Imagine pallets stacked high with drywall compound. Whenever there are walls to be patched in the home of someone who can't afford to fix them, a volunteer could stop here to pick up the drywall and then go fix the holes.

"'Imagine a pallet over there stacked high with blankets. In the winter, when the heat in people's apartments doesn't work, we could pass out blankets.'

"I was reaching for my wallet! That is vision casting. If you have the gift of leadership, God ignites in your heart a vision. You cannot not talk about it. There is so much power released when leaders start casting a godly vision. It draws people out of the woodwork. It gets bored spectators out onto the playing field."[2]

—BILL HYBELS

Moving Up to the Next Level

Earlier I mentioned a great quote that came from the *Harvard Business Review*. I said we would eventually look at it more closely, so let's take it apart and learn:

Followers want comfort, stability, and
solutions from their leaders.
But that's babysitting.
Real leaders ask hard questions and
knock people out of their comfort zones.
Then they manage the resulting distress.[3]

Offering Comfort, Stability, and Solutions

Notice that followers want three things from their leaders: comfort, stability, and solutions. Who are your followers? In a church, they're your staff and congregation. In a business, they are your customers and employees. These people will almost never ask you to be visionary, but they are certain to ask you to help make their life comfortable, stable, and problem-free.

> *When your memories are more exciting than your dreams, you've begun to die.*

Now there's nothing wrong with providing these three things. Your followers—your customers, members, employees—will love you for it! But if that's all you do, that's not leadership; it's babysitting.

If I were to lead my church that way, I would basically be a pastoral babysitter simply helping my members stay comfortable until they die and go to heaven. If I were to lead a company that way, I would be a corporate or division babysitter. And if I were to lead in my home that way as a father, my kids would never grow up and get out of the nest! It takes more to be a leader.

Knocking People Out of the Comfort Zone

Real leaders ask hard questions, then knock people out of their comfort zones. They say, "I know we're comfortable at this level. But what would happen if we stretched ourselves beyond where we've ever been before?" Great leaders set a vision that challenges people to grow. They dream about what *could* be, and motivate their people toward those goals.

Whether you lead a single child, a 1000-member church, or a Fortune 500 corporation, they all need to be challenged to go and grow beyond their yesterday. A real leader makes sure his or her followers have a dream.

This principle is illustrated in Scripture. In Hebrews 11:6, we read that without faith it is impossible to please God. And if you study Hebrews chapter 11, often called the "Hall of Faith" chapter, you'll see that faith is always about taking a risk, stretching to do something you've never done before. Hebrews 11:1 says, "Faith is the assurance of things hoped for, the conviction of things not seen." Doing what you've always done in the past does not require faith. You already know you can reach the goal and accomplish the objective. By contrast, in Hebrews 11:8, Abraham "went out, not knowing where he was going." Faith always takes you into uncharted territory. Keep your dreams more exciting than your memories. When your memories are more exciting than your dreams, you've begun to die.

Managing the Resulting Distress

Of course, after you knock your people out of their comfort zone, they will be uncomfortable for a while. Change will cause some chaos, and it's best to talk about it. When our church went from two to three services, I told our people, "We're going to have chaos on Sunday for at least a month, and don't expect all the problems to clear up right away. But eventually we'll settle into our new routines. You'll learn where to park, how to get around, and adjust to a tighter schedule. And God will use the changes to His glory and for the growth of His church. Here are some places you can go if you need help making this new plan work for your family." I also exhorted our staff, "Let's love our people through the change." Our team then went to work serving and assisting our members. We worked hard to help make the transition go as smoothly and easily as possible.

Thinking About and Adjusting Your Goals

As you imagine the future and set your goals, here are a few tips you may find helpful:

Think Bigger

First, you want to *focus on goals that, if accomplished, will make a significant difference in the growth or quality of the ministry.* Many leaders devote most of their energy toward goals that are heavy on maintenance and light on mission. Even if these goals are accomplished, they end up making very little difference in the health or growth of your ministry or organization. Always have at least one big goal that, if

> ⟨⟨⟨⟩⟩⟩
>
> "I listened to a futurist who challenged a group of us with this question: 'What is it that is impossible to do today in your industry or market, that if you could do it, it would revolutionize your business, and maybe the world?' That question stuck with me and still, to this day, stimulates my thinking."
>
> —GARY JOHNSON, CORPORATE SAFETY DIRECTOR, 40 YEARS IN MANAGEMENT AT LARGE COMPANIES, INCLUDING XEROX

accomplished, holds the potential to really move you forward.

Think Longer

Second, focus on goals that look beyond the one-year window. A common mistake is to think only in terms of what an organization wants to do this year. Your most exciting goals may be longer-term goals that take three to five years to accomplish.

Think BHAG

At our church, goals that are bigger, longer, and push your faith to the limit are called BHAGs—Bold, Hairy, Audacious Goals. I encourage every church or organization to always have one BHAG on their list of dreams. They tend to wake up the skeptics and doubters in the crowd! They are strategic initiatives that might never be accomplished. But if they are realized, they hold great potential for moving the mission forward by leaps, not mere steps. They don't just empower, they propel. You may very well find your business or church doing something far greater than you ever dared to dream before. My word to the skeptic is this:

If you dream it, I *cannot* promise you
that your dreams will be reached,
but if you fail to even dream it,
I *can* promise you it will *never* be reached.

Think Like a Reporter

Third, here is an exercise that's fun and helps leadership teams envision their future. Challenge them to write a description of themselves three to five years from now. Ask them to imagine what their church or organization will look like and put their thoughts on paper. This exercise has a way of helping your fellow leaders to visualize the future. Tell them to optimistically imagine what their department or ministry might look like if all their aspirations and dreams come true. After they finish, tell them to now write an article as if they were journalists reporting on your organization. Then ask this question: "What needs to change in order to get us moving in this direction?" Now you've given your people a way to articulate tangible goals that will motivate them to tackle the future.

Adjust the Present

Finally, as you set your vision for the future, you need to adjust the present. After all, you can't just set a new goal and add it on top of everything else you're already doing. Do you need to add staff or recruit some new volunteers to handle the extra work? What needs to be done in order to make the vision become reality? Consider this statement:

Insanity is doing the same thing over and over
and expecting different results.

If you continue to do what you've always done, you'll continue to get what you've always got. You have no reason to expect different results unless you adjust. Remember this fact of leadership when you hit a roadblock or barrier. First pray, and ask God to solve it. Then pray, and ask for wisdom to adjust.

Sometimes you need to reallocate your resources. Jim Collins, in his excellent book on what makes for successful and enduring companies, *Built to Last,* observed that strategic planning is only one aspect of healthy change. It is about 10 percent of the work, whereas issues of realignment and reallocation of resources make up the greater portion of what must be done to stay vibrant and healthy over the long haul. Unless you are in an extremely resource-rich environment, you cannot do everything. Even if you have unlimited resources, money to spend, and can afford to hire more people, *you the leader are a limited resource.* You must learn to make choices. So, you may find it wise to remember the advice I give to our staff when dreaming new goals:

Leadership Tip:

Remember to *off-load* before you *reload*
to pursue new dreams.

Personality Gift
+ Leadership

One of my common leadership mistakes in my early years was to violate this principle repeatedly. I loved to dream new dreams. I am an idea guy. I never have a shortage of new initiatives to pursue. Yet, I tended to think I could always handle just one more thing. Not true. You and I are a limited resource, so adding new responsibilities without subtracting some less important responsibility is leadership suicide. You will eventually burn yourself out. Make sure your people are free to offload as you load up with a new vision for the future.

Connecting Vision to the Inner Ring: Spirituality and Humility

Now, let's take what we've learned about vision and relate it to the inner ring qualities of humility and spirituality. How do they fit together?

Humility listens, learns, and focuses on others and is more willing to take risks. It takes humility to assess well, listen to others, and confront the truth about yourself and your mission. The humble leader, because he is not prideful, will learn quicker and tune in to the needs of the customers, staff, or congregation. And because the humble leader's ego isn't wrapped up in "what is," he is much more likely to be innovative and dream "what could be."

Spirituality, combined with vision, equips a leader with a faith in God that will embolden him to take risks when necessary. This leader knows his security is not in his personal success. His core values will serve as an anchor in an unstable business or ministry world. His decisions during tough times, or on tough issues, will not waver or pander to public opinion. His core values establish his priorities, reminding him that his loved ones matter more than his marketplace goals or ministry dreams.

This leader will sleep well at night, knowing His God is with him and his priorities are in line. He is pursuing God's big picture, a compelling vision that gives purpose to his life—purpose that goes beyond the paycheck, the bottom line of the company, or the attendance at his church. It's not about the numbers; it's about people. Therefore, he can wake up and head out the next day, refreshed and confident in who he is, what he is about, and what he needs to do to lead. Yes, he can run hard, but he can also still come home...and have a life.

LESS IS MORE Leadership:
Putting *Imagination—the Power of Vision* into Action

1. The first step to implementing the power of vision is to *assess the past* by asking, How are we *really* doing?

   My ministry's/organization's primary strengths are...

   One area in need of improvement is...

   My plan for creating a regular "feedback loop" from the people I serve is...

2. The second step is to *envision the future:* What are our dreams for the future?

   In light of the above assessment, a couple key goals for the coming year are...

   One BHAG (a Bold Hairy Audacious Goal) for us to pursue would be...

3. The third step is to *adjust the present:* What needs to change to get us moving?

> **Warning:** Insanity is doing the same thing over and over and expecting different results.

What needs to change to get us going?

What do I/we need to *off-load* in order to *reload* for these new objectives? How will this be covered if necessary?

"So then, when the Lord Jesus had spoken to them, He was received up into heaven, and sat down at the right hand of God. And they went out...."
—JESUS AT HIS FINAL LEADERSHIP MEETING (MARK 16:15-20)

"Most U.S. corporations today are over-managed and underled."[1]
—JOHN KOTTER, *HARVARD BUSINESS REVIEW*

On the top five factors for excellence:
"One would be people. Two would be people. Three would be people. Four would be people. And five would be people."[2]
—WALTER BRUCKART, FORMER VP CIRCUIT CITY

"Always Looking for Great People"[3]
—BANNER AT CIRCUIT CITY

"The trouble with a great many men is that they spread themselves out over too much ground. They fail in everything. If they would only put their life into one channel, and keep in it, they would accomplish something."[4]
—D.L. MOODY, PROMINENT CHRISTIAN LEADER

CHAPTER FIVE

Mobilization—
The Power of Letting Go

On welfare in New Jersey is not the way little boys plan to grow up. But for Todd, his three brothers and his sister, these were the cards they were dealt. Dad left years earlier and was nowhere to be found. Mom did her best, working several low-wage jobs and counting on welfare to fill the gap. It was the best this single mom could do. The family was always in survival mode throughout most of Todd's childhood. Sometime early in life, Todd decided that the poverty of his childhood would not define the rest of his life. He would break the cycle and make it, no matter what. College really wasn't even a possibility, so he focused his energy on work. At age 10 he discovered his gift for sales. By age 12, he had two jobs, working and closing his little "deals." He was off and running toward his dreams.

Twenty years later, he found himself the top salesman for a west-coast company. He ran the numbers one day and realized, "I'm making somebody a lot of money!" Sure he was well paid, but that wasn't enough. He arranged a meeting with his boss, the owner of the company, and asked, "What would it take to buy the company?" The owner smiled, laughed, and disregarded the statement. When Todd pushed, he finally gave him a number, confident that would end the discussion. Todd didn't forget the number. He mortgaged his home, pulled together all his resources, and found a partner to make up the difference. Todd told me, "Dale, it took about six months for me to close all the loops. I'll never forget the shocked look on the boss's face when

New dreams and new goals require new partners in leadership.

I showed up with all the paperwork and resources, to close his eight-figure deal and buy the company!" Todd became the owner and president of his own company! His is a classic rags-to-riches story. And this one is for real—not a fairy tale!

However, like most real-life stories, Todd's journey was not without pain. He wasn't content to just own the company. He wanted to grow it, and he did. He was good at what he did. He had dreams and visions of bigger and better things. He and his wife enjoyed the blessings of Todd's hard work and long hours—at least the financial side of the equation. Yet the more the company grew, the more time it required of Todd. And the more time Todd gave it, the more it grew. Distribution and sales were expanded coast to coast within three years. And with each expansion came more demands, more concerns, and more time on the road or in the air.

One day, Todd got a call that stopped him in his corporate tracks. The new bottom line for Todd had nothing to do with his leadership, but everything to do with his life. His marriage was in deep trouble and in desperate need of repair. His wife had lost hope. While the new company vision was being constructed and expanded, the ground under his marriage and his personal life had been steadily eroding. He knew he had to make a change. He didn't want to abandon his professional dreams, but his personal life was now becoming a nightmare. His professional success had set him up for personal failure.

At the heart of Todd's struggle was a problem common among successful leaders: How can I expand my vision and pursue new goals when I'm already out of time? Should I just keep pushing the limits and hope that somehow life will hold together? Or should I abandon the vision and give up on my dreams to have a life?

Well, there *is* a way to keep leading, keep growing, and yet not sacrifice yourself or your family on the altar of the church or the corporation. I call it the "lead more, manage less" principle. This is the discipline of *mobilization* and *the power of letting go.*

The dilemma in Todd's story is not at all uncommon. I wish it was, but I've seen it too many times. Pastors hit it every time people start responding to their messages, and the church begins to grow. If a leader hopes to continue leading with vision and still have a life, he cannot do it alone. New dreams and new goals require new partners in leadership. New volunteers or employees may bring temporary relief, but they won't help the long-term health of the leader.

The key to leading and still having a life is *mobilization,* or releasing leadership to others. When you as a leader learn to go beyond mere delegation to true mobilization, you actually *increase* your leadership potential, not decrease it. Less is more. There's less for you to manage, which means there's more of you ready and available to lead!

The "lead more, manage less" principle is good ministry sense, good business sense, and it is affirmed throughout Scripture. Here are two examples:

John 21:16—Shortly before Jesus, the Great Shepherd, ascended to heaven, He challenged Peter to go feed His sheep. Jesus passed His shepherding responsibility on to Peter, one of His key young leaders. Shortly thereafter He gathered His leaders on a mountaintop and ascended to heaven in their very presence. Talk about letting go!

2 Timothy 2:2—The apostle Paul mobilized his young protégé, Timothy, and encouraged him to lead and raise up other leaders. Paul knew the secret to leadership success was not in "sucking it up and working at all hours to get everything done." Paul had trained Timothy to lead, and Timothy, in turn, was to train others. The goal was the multiplication of leaders:

> The things which you have heard from me
> in the presence of many witnesses,
> entrust these to faithful men
> who will be able to teach others also (2 Timothy 2:2).

Notice the progression here:

- *"The things you heard from me"* —Paul to Timothy, a second generation leader

- *"entrust to faithful men"* —Timothy to a third generation of leaders

- *"who will be able to teach others also"* —third generation of leaders to a fourth!

Paul's words outline for us the principle of spiritual multiplication— the mobilization of new disciples and new leaders. His vision went beyond the mere transfer of knowledge; he was committed to raising up a new generation of teachers and leaders who would go on to pass the baton to others. Too many leaders today hold onto their positions tenaciously and fear those who rise to their level, viewing them as potential threats. But an effective leader is one who wants to nurture others to greater heights of leadership.

Leadership Tip:
The goal of the servant leader is to lead others
not only into *service* but into *leadership.*

Most of us are very comfortable with merely exhorting our followers to serve. In a church, for example, we often say, "Every one of you needs to serve in ministry somewhere." When we do that, we overlook the fact that we not only need people who can serve, we desperately need people who can lead, too. *Whether in a business or a ministry, you have had times when what you really needed was not more servants, but more leaders.* We need those who are motivated to go after new goals and make them happen! To empower an organization forward, you need not only a compelling vision or goals that *energize* the troops, you also need leaders to *organize* those troops and turn the vision into reality. If you try to take your business or ministry to a higher level without letting go of some of your own leadership responsibilities, you will load yourself up then burn yourself out before you realize it! Remember, less is more, so slow down and mobilize a team of leaders.

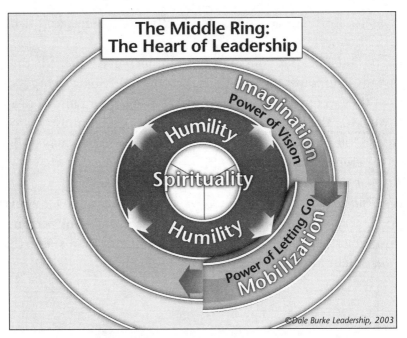

The Process of Mobilization

How do you motivate people and mobilize them to lead with you? Here are three suggestions to keep in mind: let them dream, let them do it, and then let them go!

Let them dream with you. When people are involved in the dreaming side of leadership with you, they are much more likely to get excited and help lead. The problem in too many companies and churches is that one leader does all the leading and simply expects *others* to serve. The leader ends up doing all the dreaming. He puts the vision together, decides where to go, and determines how to get there. The followers are simply recruited to carry out the vision of the leader—to accomplish *his dreams*. Your team is much more likely to be excited about "doing the work" if you let them "dream the dream." Get them involved as you talk about the problem, cast the vision, and imagine what "could be." Then let them come up with ideas and solutions—the best ways to accomplish the desired end. In fact, if there's a conference you could attend to train yourself for a particular task, instead of going yourself, send a couple "high octane" leaders in your place. You know, the kind with high potential for getting a job done. Let them learn, let them get motivated by the conference, and debrief with them when they return. Then...

Let them do it. After your staff or volunteers have helped "dream the dream," empower them with the responsibility of carrying it out. Because they were involved from the beginning, their sense of ownership will be off the charts! Now they'll take their job or ministry responsibility seriously. Now you are mobilizing other leaders who will be eager to serve and sacrifice to get it done. Why? Because they're not doing *your* thing, they're doing *their* thing.

Let them go. After you've given away the task, leave your workers alone. Be their cheerleader, their encourager, their point person for resources. But the job is theirs. The ministry is theirs. Entrust it to them and turn them loose!

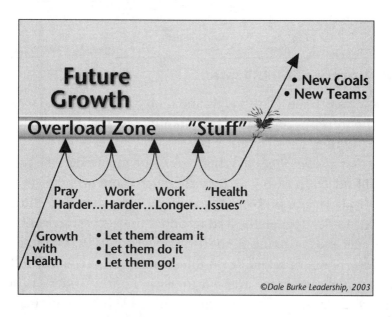

©Dale Burke Leadership, 2003

You say, "But, Dale, I've got the training and experience. I can do it better than they can." That may be true, but let me suggest you follow what I call the 80-percent rule. When someone else, or a even a team of "someone elses," can do the job 80 percent as well as you can do it, let it go, unless it's your "main thing." You'll get most of the gain you need, and over time, they will get better and better.

Eventually, they will probably do the job better than you could do! Why? Because it will become their "main thing." And it's best for you as a leader to let go and stay focused on *your* "main thing"—your area of unique giftedness. Letting go is good for everyone. Less is more.

〈〈〈〉〉〉

I have a problem with always wanting to be the "firefighter"! When something goes wrong, or there is a need, my tendency is to push through to the front line with my "fire hose" in hand and want to take over and fix it for everybody else. The problem is that no one else learns how to fight the fire, and if I'm not around and a "fire" starts, things burn down! I have learned that when I relax and let others "fight the fire," most of the time, they come up with a better way of putting it out. But it is hard to not "grab that fire hose" when I see a fire starting.

—GARY JOHNSON, CORPORATE SAFETY DIRECTOR,
40 YEARS IN MANAGEMENT AT LARGE COMPANIES,
INCLUDING XEROX

The Difference Between Leading and Managing

One reason leaders struggle with letting go is their failure to grasp the essence of true leadership. Understanding the difference between leading and managing is vital for today's busy leader, especially if the organization is to continue growing. John Kotter, in an excellent article in *Harvard Business Review*, wrote:

Most U.S. corporations today are over-managed and underled.[5]

While Kotter is speaking of corporate America, his statement applies to churches as well. If you want your company or church to grow, you must instill the vision and values, find the right people, then get out of the way and let them dream, let them do it, and let them go. Only then will you find yourself leading more and managing less. Don't succumb to the temptation to micromanage your people. That's not letting go. You must learn to let go and give your team real freedom and the opportunity to make their own decisions. That's what LESS IS MORE Leadership is all about—mobilizing a team of leaders so that you can both lead and have a life.

You might be surprised to know that even in Jesus' launching of the church we can see the difference between leading and managing. A wonderful example of the "lead more, manage less" principle is found in the Great Commission. Jesus said, "Go therefore and make disciples of all the nations" (Matthew 28:19). In essence, He promised to be with them, to support and care for them, but He trusted His young leaders and handed His mission over to them. He said, "Now go for it!" and then He left.

Now, we know that Jesus sent the Holy Spirit to empower and guide His workers. But still, Jesus left the scene. He literally turned everything over to His group of followers. He said, "You know the message; you have the assignment; you know the mission. Now go do it."

What's more, Jesus didn't leave any policy manuals or business plans for them. He left no sample worship services or discipleship notebooks. Yet the disciples were equipped with the *values* and *vision* of Jesus and His kingdom. As to methodology, techniques, and style, it was up to them to figure those out. Jesus would guide them, but from a distance. While it's true that God guides the life of a leader, He doesn't micromanage through a leader. God cares primarily about the vision and values of His movement and the character of His leaders, but He has given them a tremendous amount of freedom to create, innovate, and explore new ways to get the job done.

In spite of the fact Jesus didn't leave any manuals or guidebooks, the church got off to a great start. The apostles may have thought, *How should we accomplish the mission?* They knew the basic essentials as modeled in Acts 2:41–47. They were devoted to teaching, praying, communion, and gathering together. Everyone took care of each other like family. And the result? God was adding to their number daily. Jesus had given tremendous flexibility to the apostles. He led them, yet didn't manage them. He imparted His vision and values, clarified the mission or goal, and let them go.

> "Most U.S. corporations today are over-managed and underled."
> —John P. Kotter
>
> | LEADERS | MANAGERS |
> |---|---|
> | Vision | Organization |
> | What could be | What is |
> | Align people | Assign people |
> | Motivate people | Control People |
>
> Based on and adapted from John P. Kotter article in
> *Harvard Business Review,* December 2001

John Kotter, in his *Harvard Business Review* article, provides a tremendously helpful summary of the difference between leading and managing. It captures exactly what Jesus was doing as a leader.

Leaders focus on *vision*. Managers focus on *organization*. Leaders focus on *what could be*, managers focus on *what is*. Leaders focus on *aligning* people—that is, they get everyone moving in the same direction to accomplish the same goal. Managers focus on *assigning* people—they find people to do the work and assign them to what needs to get done. Leaders focus on *motivating* people, while managers *control* people. I'm not talking about an unhealthy control; people do need to be told where to go, what to do, and how to do it. But leaders are more hands-off, and managers are more hands-on.

Is Leadership for Everyone?

As we look at the differences between leading and managing, realize that I'm not saying we don't need good managers. Never fail to appreciate a gifted manager. Every leader knows how essential they are. Without good managers, chaos would be the order of the day! And

God does call some people to simply serve—to do a job and do it well as a servant. We all know that many servants are needed to help move any mission forward. What we're addressing here is the fact a leader should be careful not to get caught up in too much management. A leader is responsible for the health and growth of the organization. In order to adapt and keep up with a fast-paced world and changing demands, you must be able to mobilize, and then let go. You can't do it all yourself, or you won't have time to think about future goals and growth. Remember, God's will is for you to lead and still have a life that honors Him!

The more freedom you give people, the more energized and excited they will become.

To find people you can mobilize, you want to keep your eyes and ears open for latent leaders disguised as humble servants or managers. The best servant-leaders always excel at serving. They faithfully fulfill their responsibilities with joy. You can count on them. As a leader, value and appreciate these gems! A faithful servant or employee is worth his or her weight in gold. Don't make him or her a manager or leader unless it's a good fit, or you will take away his or her real joy—just doing a job with excellence.

Some of your best servants will become model managers, showing an ability to organize, deal with "what is," and assign the work to willing servants in the church and workplace. They love bringing order out of chaos, building teams, solving problems. When you recognize these management gifts, nurture them. Let them manage. A good manager is worth his weight in platinum! Actually, a good servant, manager, and leader are *all* worth more than you can imagine. God's will for each one is that they simply step up and give their best in whatever role they tackle. Each one is uniquely gifted, and God wants us as leaders to value every member of the team.

But ultimately, you as a leader need to lead more and manage less. You need to get your team together, clarify the challenge, and say, "You have the freedom to do whatever you believe works best to get the job done. Just keep in mind our commitment to our core values and the vision that define us." Define the mission, and let them design the methods. The more freedom you give people, the more energized and excited they will become. I guarantee it.

Connecting Mobilization to the Inner Ring

As we learned earlier, the four disciplines in the middle circle of leadership need to be firmly rooted in the two disciplines of the inner ring. Now that we understand what mobilization—or "lead more, manage less"—is all about, let's see how it relates to the leader's humility and spirituality. Once again, we will see that stable convictions and a humble attitude are essential to great mobilization.

> ≪ ≺ ≻ ≫
>
> "Stripped to its essentials, leadership involves just three things—a leader, followers, and a common goal."[6]
>
> —WARREN BENNIS AND
> ROBERT THOMAS

Remember my friend Todd? He had never anchored his life in authentic spirituality. His wife went to church, but he didn't have the time or the interest. His personal crisis got his attention, and he began to listen and learn. Todd Williams, the president of Continental Western Corporation, is one of my good friends and an endorser of this book. Today Todd is doing great—at work, at home, and as a committed follower of Christ. He has gone through an exciting yet difficult transition in how he approaches both life and leadership. He still leads with vision, and still loves closing a deal as a marketplace competitor. But his priorities are now realigned. After attending the LESS IS MORE Leadership seminar for Christian business executives, he wrote:

> Dear Dale,
>
> As a business leader in the marketplace, I constantly was challenged to find some balance in my life. It seemed like the more success I had, the harder I worked, and the longer I worked, the greater the challenges. My world was a fast-paced marketplace, with a constant sense of overload. Deadlines could not be ignored, integrity was constantly tested, and moral temptations were commonplace. I

needed some help finding balance. The LESS IS MORE Leadership sessions showed me that even business leaders need to be anchored in spirituality through a relationship with Christ and a commitment to His core values. Thanks for giving me the core skills and values of successful leadership. It has given me back some margin in my life! I now know I can be an effective, growing leader in a competitive market and not lose myself, or my marriage, in the process. Thanks!

Todd Williams

President, Continental Western Corporation

By the way, Todd's mother is now gone; she died of a heart attack in 2001. But before she died, Todd had the joy of buying her the house she grew up in as a child, which had been built by her own father.

Mobilization and Humility

Humility is an essential quality for anyone who wants to lead more and manage less. Humility comes into play in relation to three key issues as a leader lets go:

The Issue of Control—What does a prideful leader do? He likes to be in control. The humble leader, by contrast, finds it easier to let go, to give away control. Now, it can be risky giving control over to the members of your church or to staff or volunteers in your company. But there's no other way to successfully keep yourself from becoming overloaded. You need to raise up others to help carry the workload with you. Prepare the hearts of your leaders, your associates, your followers by teaching them the right core values and vision, and eventually you will be able to turn them loose and watch them run... without fearing where they may end up!

The Issue of Credit—We all crave getting praise for a job well done, don't we? We enjoy getting people's accolades; we love to get the credit. But being a humble leader means giving up control, which usually means giving up the credit as well. It's hard for us to watch someone else get the praise for something we used to do. But it's for the good of the organization—and your own leadership. The wise leader knows he can't do it all. And it takes humility to turn that realization into reality. Ralph Waldo Emerson is quoted as having said,

There is no limit
to what can be accomplished
when no one cares
who gets the credit.

‹‹‹ ›››

"In a world where I am continually confronted with multiple books to read, messages to prepare, meetings to attend, people to call and visit, staff to manage, if I didn't learn to let things go, I would drown and take a lot of people down with me."

—ROY FRUITS

Other great leaders, such as John Wooden of UCLA fame, have reaffirmed and modeled this vital truth. If it's not about you, you can let go, watch it grow, and then go have a life! Less is more.

The Issue of Competence—A humble leader is willing to give up a responsibility to someone who might not, at least initially, do the job quite as well. You may be more competent, but if you keep trying to control and do everything, you will limit your ability to grow as an organization and as a leader. Remember the 80-percent principle: If someone else can do the work at least 80 percent as well as you can, then be willing to give up control, give over the credit, and accept the competence level that may be a notch or two below your personal best. And when you do, you will gain new leaders with growing competencies that eventually excel beyond your expectations.

Mobilization and Spirituality

It takes more than humility to let go and let others lead with you. It also takes spiritual strength and convictions. Here's why:

Letting Go Can Be Lonely—When you're leading and communicating a vision to others and motivating them to come up with ideas and carry them out, that means you're doing less hands-on managing. And that, in turn, means you're not around some people quite as much as you used to be as the hands-on manager. So in that sense, leadership can be lonely. You must know that what you are doing is the will of your one Master. You must be convinced that mobilization is a core value of God's approach to leadership. Empowering others to lead must be a part of your overall vision for your life. And if you value people, you will

> *Nothing feels better than seeing a vision that you helped birth be passed on into the capable hands of others.*

want to see them blossom and become the leaders God wants them to be. Well defined values and vision help make letting go a joy!

Letting Go Requires Learning—You'll find yourself constantly stretched as a leader because setting a vision and mobilizing people requires you to chart new territory. You're always going somewhere you've never been before. Dreaming about "what could be" doesn't just come naturally. It's work. And when you're spiritually stable and strong, you'll be in a better position to learn new skills. You will be listening to the voice of God to discern what the next dream should be. You will be learning how to keep stretching the organization without destroying your personal and family life. You must be a lifelong learner to keep adapting your own leadership and not just settle down.

Leadership Is Hard Work—Sometimes managing is easier than leading. That may sound strange, but it's true. It's easy for a leader to decide, "I'll go ahead and do it myself because it's easier for me to just take care of it rather than to teach someone else how to do it." It takes more effort to pass a vision on to others and then equip them to carry it out. While it's true that imparting vision to others is hard work on the front end, once you've equipped and mobilized faithful leaders, it's out of your hands. There might be more work for you up front, but after handing it off, your work is done. So, it's well worthwhile to get the right person or team in place and let go. Nothing feels better than seeing a vision that you helped birth be passed on into the capable hands of others to the extent that you no longer have to even think about it. You know it's going to be done well. You have the joy of watching the organization move forward. Your people are growing into real leadership roles and loving it! And plus, it's no longer on your to-do list. That's why it's always to your advantage to lead more and manage less.

So where are we now? In the middle ring of leadership, advancing the mission always starts with imagination—the power of vision. Then as we adopt new goals, we can't keep trying to cover all the bases ourselves. That brings us to the need to mobilize other leaders—to raise up new leadership to take responsibility for the new vision. And that, ultimately, will free up time for you as a leader...so that you can continue to make the best use of your time. And that's the topic of the next chapter. What is God's will for you, the leader with a little more time? Enjoy a break? Take a vacation? Sure, why not! But what about when you are on the job? Try "less is more," the discipline of specialization—maximizing your unique abilities.

For Some.

LESS IS MORE Leadership:
Putting *Mobilization—the Power of Letting Go* into Action

> *Leadership Tip:* The goal of the servant-leader is to lead others not only into *service* but into *leadership*.

1. What will you and your team do this year to expand your leadership base to support healthy growth?

2. What area of "managing" you would like to release to others so you can free yourself to "lead more"?

3. When and where will you *lead more* and *manage less*?

   (Note: Review the difference between the two.)

4. My plan for encouraging and equipping my current team of managers and leaders is...

5. My plan for communicating core values and vision on a regular basis is...

"Globally, only 20 percent of employees...
feel their strengths are in play every day."[1]

—GALLUP POLL OF 1.7 MILLION PEOPLE, AS CITED
IN *NOW, DISCOVER YOUR STRENGTHS*

"I have come down from heaven, not to do My own will,
but the will of Him who sent Me."

—JESUS (JOHN 6:38)

"What you are is God's gift to you;
what you do with yourself is your gift to God."

—DANISH PROVERB

"We are all talented people.
Anything whereby we may glorify God is a talent."

—J.C. RYLE, NINETEENTH-CENTURY MINISTER AND WRITER

"God has different kinds of work to do;
and since He chooses to employ men,
He has need of different kinds of instruments."

—THOMAS GUTHRIE, NINETEENTH-CENTURY SCOTTISH MINISTER
AND SOCIAL REFORMER

CHAPTER SIX

Specialization—
The Power of Unique Abilities

———

Jim Seybert, an ideation consultant (definition: a really creative person who loves to help others get out of the box and discover creative solutions) once wrote, "Have you ever seen a grizzly bear catch a fish? Or a cheetah stalk and run down her prey? Both of these predators are crystal-clear examples of the strength we find when we know what we're good at and concentrate on doing it."[2]

In fact, every creature on the planet is a unique display of God's grand design. Their very survival depends on their willingness to recognize and do something really well. For the animal kingdom, awareness of unique ability seems to come naturally. They are born with it; we call it *instinct*. From the time they come out of the womb, they get it, accept it, and get going. Only in cartoons and fairy tales do animals wish they could be something else and refuse to act on their unique abilities. The one who does refuse falls into another category in the animal kingdom—*extinct*. Only human beings, made in the image of God, are truly free to explore a vast array of possibilities for their lives. To some degree, every individual person, and leader, is a one-of-a-kind creature!

Therefore, behind every person is a God-ordained purpose. And God is shaping every one of His children to play their part in His plan.

> *There's absolutely no room for pride when we remember that the source of all our giftedness is God, and not ourselves.*

You, as a Christian leader, are one of those unique creations by God. You are who you are for a reason. You are where you are for a reason. You have been and continue to be crafted by God, shaped and molded by forces great and small, visible and invisible. From the smallest bits of your DNA to the greatest experiences of your life, you are continually being crafted into a one-of-a-kind model of God's handiwork. As the psalmist said, you are fearfully and wonderfully made (Psalm 139:14). Or, as I once saw on a poster, "God Don't Make No JUNK!"

Jesus, our role-model leader, knew who He was and why He was here, and built His life and leadership around these facts. He was a person with a purpose. He lived not to do "whatever came His way," but to fulfill the mission His heavenly Father had designed Him to fulfill. "I have come...not to do My own will, but the will of Him who sent Me," said Jesus (John 6.38).

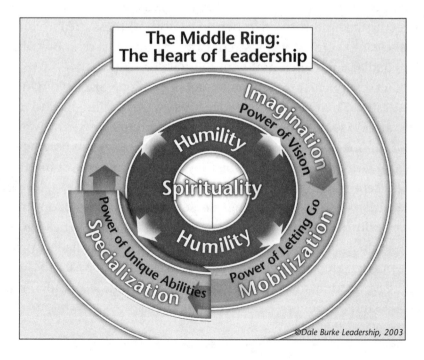

The Middle Ring: The Heart of Leadership

Imagination — Power of Vision

Humility

Spirituality

Humility

Specialization — Power of Unique Abilities

Mobilization — Power of Letting Go

©Dale Burke Leadership, 2003

Unique for a Purpose

Every person, including every leader, has a unique combination of skills and experiences that makes him or her a specialist of some kind. This is especially true of Christians, who also have a spiritual giftedness specially endowed by God. Scripture affirms this, yet it is an often-overlooked fact of life:

> Now there are varieties of gifts, but the same Spirit.
> And there are varieties of ministries, and the same Lord. There are
> varieties of effects, but the same God who works all things
> in all persons. But to *each one* is given the manifestation
> of the Spirit for the common good (1 Corinthians 12:4-7).

Our giftedness is meant for "the common good" of others in the church. And each of us is unique in our giftedness for a purpose. God's design is not for everyone to be doing "whatever," but for each one of us to serve in keeping with our one-of-a-kind set of gifts and abilities.

Romans 12:3-6 lays out some divine advice for every person who wants to maximize their personal touch on history. These five "Be" phrases are especially useful to the busy, overloaded leader in search of his or her unique purpose in life:

1. *Be Humble*—"I say to everyone among you not to think more highly of himself than he ought to think" (verse 3). Don't be prideful as you identify or use your gifts. God deserves the credit for who you are and what you do. Remember the power of humility!

2. *Be Wise*—"think so as to have sound judgment" (verse 3). Think objectively. Be honest with yourself and know yourself well—both your strengths and your weaknesses. Remember, the truth is always your ally, never your enemy. Assessment starts with yourself!

3. *Be Unique*—"all the members do not have the same function" (verse 4). A leader should not be doing everything that comes along. If he tries, with a servant spirit, to do everything people want him to do, he might please his people, but he will likely displease God, His Master, who has gifted him for a specific task.

4. *Be Appreciative*—"we have gifts that differ according to the grace given to us" (verse 6). Whatever kind or combination of giftedness you have as a leader, it is your personal gift from God. He makes no mistakes when He's putting His gift list together! And it has nothing to do with whether you've been "naughty or nice." In fact, it is labeled a "grace" gift, one you did nothing to earn or deserve. There's absolutely no room for pride when we remember that the source of all our giftedness is God, and not ourselves.

5. *Be Focused*—"each of us is to exercise them accordingly...if service, in his serving; or he who teaches, in his teaching...he who leads, with diligence" (verses 6-8). God's desire is for us to focus our efforts on whatever He has uniquely gifted and custom-designed for us to do. Romans 12:6 says we're to use our unique ability "with diligence." So, pour yourself into what God has designed you to do. Less really is more, isn't it?!

Now, we must also keep in mind Jesus' words, "Whoever wishes to become great...shall be [a] servant" (Matthew 20:26). We're to get down and care for our people. We're to consider their needs more important than our own. We learned in chapter 3 that we are to think and lead with a servant attitude, and that humility is a powerful force for leadership. This truth surfaces a point of tension for us as leaders. On the one hand, we're to stay focused on our area of unique giftedness. On the other, we're to be willing to help others. How can we achieve the right balance between utilizing our unique abilities and serving others? Here's the key: Be willing, on occasion, to serve wherever needed. Keep a "no job is beneath me" attitude. If a real need arises, and you have some time, then jump in and be a servant—help out! Yet always keep your calling as your first priority.

Leadership Tip:
You will serve your people best
when you lead from your unique abilities.

You must never allow yourself to get so focused on responding to people's felt needs that you ignore their real need—the need for you, the leader, to lead from your strengths. If you as the leader begin to compromise your "main things" (that is, activities that are mission-critical, top priority, or utilize your unique abilities) in order to deal with tasks other people should do, you will hurt the health and growth of your entire organization. This is why it is crucial for you as a leader to set aside quality "results time" in your schedule so you can focus on your "main thing" without feeling rushed all the time. In a later chapter I'll show you how to protect time for results when we discuss concentration—*the power of focus* in the "Execution" ring of leadership.

An undeniable fact of leadership is this: to accomplish *more*, you need to do *less*. If you want to expand, you must learn to shrink—constantly downsizing your personal to-do list. To carry greater responsibility as a leader, you must learn to play fewer roles. In a nutshell...

Specialization doesn't mean you are *doing less;*
in fact, you are *doing more.*
But you're doing more of your *best* stuff
instead of *just* stuff.

The Need to Specialize

As the early church expanded, the leaders became busy and quickly came to realize their need to specialize. Because the organization was growing and there were new "clients" to care for along with new problems and needs, the leaders couldn't keep up with it all. Before long, some people began to complain, "Our needs aren't being met." Notice what happened next:

> Now at this time while the disciples were increasing in number, a complaint arose...widows were being overlooked in the daily serving of food. So the twelve [leaders] summoned the congregation...and said, "Therefore, brethren,

select from among you seven men of good reputation...
whom we may put in charge of this task. But we will devote
ourselves to prayer and to the ministry of the word."... The
statement found approval with the whole congregation....
The word of God kept on spreading; and the number of the
disciples continued to increase greatly (Acts 6:1-7).

These leaders had a real problem: growth! God was blessing their
efforts with results and more followers. The business equivalent would
be not having enough product to keep up with the demand. You have
too many customers, and as a result, you need to expand your staff
and production capabilities.

Notice how the church leaders in Acts 6 solved the problem:

- They *listened* and faced reality—widows were being overlooked.

- They showed they *cared*—they "summoned the congregation."

- They *mobilized* a new team, with new leaders to manage it—"select
  seven from among you...whom we may put in charge of this task."

- They *stayed focused* on their main thing—"It is not desirable for
  us to neglect the word of God in order to serve tables."

- The *people were pleased* with the plan—"The statement found
  approval."

- The *numbers kept on increasing*— "The Word of God kept spreading;
  and the number of the disciples continued to increase greatly."

It is important for every leader, at every level, to be compassionate
and really care. Yet you must also be careful as you strategize to meet
these needs.

Leadership Tip:
The leader must own the responsibility to *fix it*
without attempting to always *be the fix*.

Leaders who feel the need to fix everything themselves will soon
face much more serious problems than the very ones they are fixing!

By focusing only on "what is" and not "what could be" (managing instead of leading), growth will grind to a halt and stagnation will soon follow. The apostles, in Acts 6, *mobilized* new leaders and experienced the power of letting go. They got others involved in solving the problem and then returned their focus to their "main thing" that they were uniquely called and gifted to do. As a result, the health and growth of the movement was protected, and its expansion continued.

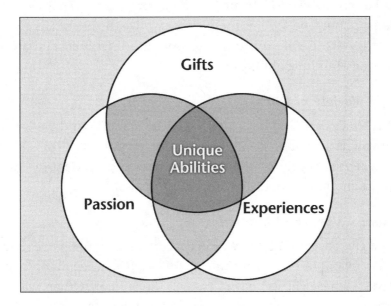

Discovering Your Unique Abilities

In 1 Corinthians 12, when Paul talks about spiritual gifts, we discover that "there are varieties of *gifts*" (verse 4). We're all gifted differently. However, we also discover "there are varieties of *ministries*" and "there are varieties of *effects*" (verses 5-6). So we have varieties of *gifts, ministries,* and *effects.*

When you consider all three elements, it becomes all the more evident just how unique each one of us is. We're gifted differently, we have different areas of passion or ministry that we care about, and we've all experienced the unique effects of those being put into operation. When you lead or serve in the zone where all three elements overlap, you are in the zone of your *unique abilities*. That is, you are not only serving in the area of your gifting, but also in the realm that you're *passionate about* and in which you have valuable *life experience*. When you lead, work, or serve in this zone—where all three elements converge—you will function at your maximum potential and offer your greatest value. Now, there will be times when we will need to serve outside of this "zone of unique abilities" because something simply must get done—even if it's not your gift or passion. That's servant-leadership! But God's will is for us to maximize the use of His gifts. So make the best use of your time by serving primarily in and around your zone of unique abilities.

Gifts: A Variety of Gifts

It is a fact that God has given you spiritual gifts, and He has also given you natural abilities. If you have certain gifts or skills, wouldn't it make sense for you to spend as much time as possible using them? It's just a matter of good stewardship of your abilities.

Passion: A Variety of Ministries

God gives every leader a passion for certain areas of service or ministry. For example, God gifts some people for teaching, but only some of those teachers will also have a passion for children. Others will have a passion for adults, or small groups, or leading others in worship. So if you're gifted to teach, God wants you not only to be a teacher, but also for you to serve in the area of your passion. The same principle applies in the workplace. Certain leaders have a passion for certain types of careers or businesses. Over the course of your life, look to discover and invest your time serving in an area you enjoy and care about. You will be surprised how much more fun leadership can be!

Experiences: A Variety of Effects

If God allows you to go through a particular experience, does He want you to use that, or ignore it? Second Corinthians 1:3-7 describes how God comforts us in our trials so that we may be equipped to comfort others "with the comfort with which we ourselves are comforted by God" (verse 4). I call this the "stewardship of experience." God doesn't waste a single experience in our lives, but uses them to shape us and make us more effective servants and leaders. It makes sense that God wants us serving and leading as much as possible from our experience base. Look at every life experience, especially painful ones, as an opportunity to grow and mature. It is usually the painful lessons that stretch and develop your leadership.

> ⟨⟨⟨⟩⟩⟩
>
> "Think of excellence as *maximizing God's endowment in you.*"[3]
>
> —JOHN BRADLEY AND JAY CARTY

Your Zone of Unique Abilities

When we lead from within any of the three circles, we are a *good* leader. When we engage in an activity that involves two of these circles, such as our giftedness and our passion, we are a *better* leader. Yet when we serve our team from the zone that represents our gifts, our passions, *and* our experiences, we are at our very *best* as a leader. I believe we can safely conclude that God's will for us as leaders is for us to lead, whenever possible, from this zone. Otherwise, we are wasting the full leadership potential entrusted to us by God.

Moving Toward the Zone

So how do we move ourselves toward this zone in which we make the most of our uniqueness? If you don't consciously make an effort to shift toward this zone, you're underutilizing what God has entrusted to you. Consider the diagram on the next page:

Each circle and star represents an activity that needs to happen for your business or church to stay healthy and continue growing. If I were to overlay your life and your abilities on this circle, you would find that some of those activities line up with your unique abilities. There are some you would be great at doing, some you would merely be okay at doing, and finally, in the outer ring, some you need to avoid altogether!

Now, when you first go into a ministry or launch a new business venture, this circle represents your zone of activity.

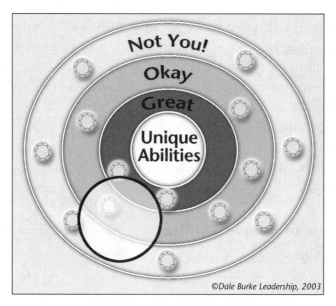

©Dale Burke Leadership, 2003

This is what you look like when you start a new venture. I know, because I've been there. In my first church, as a solo pastor, I did everything from unlocking the doors to fixing the overflowing toilet! You take care of whatever has to be done. There's nothing wrong with that...at first. But that is not God's will for you in the long haul. One of the serious mistakes leaders and pastors make is they think God's will is for them to enlarge their circle and try to accomplish more as their business or ministry grows (as below).

©Dale Burke Leadership, 2003

So they pray harder, work harder, and work longer hours to solve their problems and keep up with the growth. But remember, God has gifted you, given you passions, and allowed specific experiences in your life in order for you to fulfill what *He* wants you to do. He's not expecting you to expand your personal circle or amount of time—especially if you are already putting in all the time you should as you balance your job with your other priorities in life. Rather, you are to shift your "circle of activity" as much as possible toward your zone of unique abilities. Don't grow it—start moving it!

©Dale Burke Leadership, 2003

As time passes, your zone of unique abilities will change somewhat as your gifts develop, your passions shift, or new experiences accumulate. At least once a year you should step back and ask two vitally important questions: 1) "God, what am I learning about my unique abilities? How are they taking shape?" And 2) "What can I do this next year to shift my 'circle,' my personal roles and responsibilities, toward the area in which I can make maximum use of my unique abilities? What can I give up so that I can focus more on my areas of giftedness and passion and experience?" If you take the time to make periodic adjustments, you'll be surprised at how much more effective you will soon become as a leader.

©Dale Burke Leadership, 2003

Two Warnings

First warning: *Be patient!* This is a lifelong process for everyone, especially leaders. It takes years to discover the nature of and range of your unique abilities. Plus, remember that God is never finished with you. You are still under construction until you die! So expect the target to shift a bit as you move through life. The goal is for you to keep shifting yourself, a little more every year, toward the center.

A second caution: *Be accountable.* Unless you own the company, don't shift your "circle of responsibilities" without checking with the boss or board. There is a word for employees who violate this rule—*unemployed!* So remember your accountability and team structure. Before you make a major shift, check with your leadership board and get their support and approval. *No surprises* is the rule. We all work under someone's leadership, so respect it. You are paid to do a job, or as a volunteer, there are certain expectations of you. So before you decide, "That's not my gift; I'm not doing it," make sure that what needs to get done will still get done.

Knowing Your Limits

Now, you may be saying, "Who's going to do that job or ministry in the outer circle—that job I really shouldn't be doing?" Well, there is someone else out there who really *should* be doing it because it's *his or her unique ability*. I can give you illustration after illustration of people who were ideally suited for taking care of those tasks that can burden a leader and distract him or her from "the main thing."

For example, at our first church, we had no janitor. In fact, we built our own building, and I helped construct it. It is a miracle it is still standing, knowing my handyman skills! A couple times I tried to fix plumbing problems, but I soon learned that water is smarter than me and very elusive. I'll never forget the day that Ralph Jones, a university professor, walked into my office and saw me trying to fix one of the toilets. He said, "Dale, what in the world are you doing trying to fix that toilet?" Then he added, "You may not know this, but on my day off, I love to work around the house. I spend all week in the midst of academia, but when the weekend comes, give me a wrench! Here's the deal: I don't want you ever to touch another piece of plumbing again. Besides, you are destroying that toilet! Look, I *can't* teach the Bible, but I *can* do plumbing. So you leave the plumbing to me, and you focus on God's Word." I don't have to tell you I was more than willing to let him have the wrench!

When my family left that church to move to California, we received a quilt from the congregation as a going-away present. Some of the families in the church made quilt blocks that had special handwork on them that represented something about our relationship to those specific families. Ralph Jones was the only man who made his own quilt block, and on that block is a plunger. That quilt is proudly displayed in our house, and every time people see it, they ask about the block with the plunger. So I'll tell them the story about Ralph Jones and his place of unique service in my former church. Not only had Ralph been serving the church, but me as well. May the Ralph Joneses of the world multiply!

When you do a job someone else ought to do, you are robbing a person of an opportunity to work or serve in his or her areas of unique abilities. So, lead more and manage less. Stay on your main thing, and let others have the opportunity to make use of their God-given gifts.

Specialization and the Inner Ring

Up to now, as we've examined each principle in the middle ring of leadership, we've seen the importance of staying connected to the inner ring—the heart of the leader. Where do humility and spirituality come into play as the leader seeks to specialize and lead from his or her unique abilities?

Specialization and Humility

It takes humility to focus on what God has equipped you to do best and release the rest to other people. You'll find it much easier to focus on your zone of unique abilities when you're humble because...

> ⟨⟨ ⟨ ⟩ ⟩⟩
>
> "When I am allowed to focus on my areas of strength or abilities it not only makes my work more enjoyable, but more productive as well. When a team is allowed to do this, it enhances the respect everyone on the team has for each other because the focus is on the strengths each person brings to the whole. This also then gives me permission to ask for help in areas where a team member is stronger and allows me to serve the team from my areas of strength. Everyone wins!"
>
> —DIRECTOR OF REWARDS AND RECOGNITION, A LARGE CATHOLIC HEALTH SYSTEM IN SOUTHERN CALIFORNIA

First, a humble leader will admit and accept his own limitations. When you're able to say, "I'm not good at these things," then you'll put those things into more capable hands.

Second, a humble leader will acknowledge and celebrate the strengths of others. He will lift up others and let them know how valuable they are to the church or organization. Prideful leaders, by contrast, want all the credit. So they take control, get the credit and praise, and then complain about being overworked!

Third, a humble leader is willing to give up taking credit for projects that once earned him praise. I believe many of us have more of our egos wrapped up in our leadership than we would ever admit. That's why we find it so hard to let go of some of our tasks. When we're humble, we won't struggle with giving up our "okay" roles, even some "great" roles, to someone else. By letting go, we allow ourselves to focus our energy more toward the center of our unique abilities.

Specialization and Spirituality

We also need spiritual strength and core convictions to help us better focus on maximizing our unique abilities. That's because...

You may be criticized and misunderstood. When you have clear convictions, core values, and are listening to God's voice, you will be less driven to have to please everyone. Some of your staff or congregation may not understand your efforts to move more toward the zone of your unique abilities. They may have different ideas about what you ought to be doing. This is why it is critical for you to be accountable to your leadership as you shift your circle toward the center and change your priorities. I tell pastors, "Make sure your priorities are affirmed by your board; then they can help shield you from criticism." It's great when, in awkward situations where others tell you how you should do your job, you can say, "I'd love to help with that, but our board [or my boss] has clearly told me to let others handle that. Let me put you in touch with the right people."

You must make sure all the essential tasks are still covered. The leader has to make sure that the tasks in the outer circle still get done. And that's work. It takes time to recruit and train someone else to respond to the needs of the "widows who are not being fed" in your organization. The easy route is simple: just do it yourself. Take care of "what is," and

> *If you have a desire to please God...you will do what it takes to specialize.*

don't worry about not having time to advance the mission. But as we've already seen, this approach is not good for the company or your leadership. Stagnation will soon follow. If you have solid convictions, a vision for investing in others, and a desire to please God more than

Key Trap

people, you will do what it takes to specialize. After all, it is a mandate from your eternal CEO!

Your future and your potential members or customers will never demand your attention, because they don't even exist yet. Or, at least they aren't around yet to complain! So everyone will be happy, at least temporarily. But remember, your present will define your future. If you don't work now to invest in your future, you will not have one. Though it's not easy to find and train others to take on whatever tasks you release, in the long run, you'll find yourself carrying less so that you can carry more.

It's easier, of course, to simply care for "what is" and forget "what could be," and to settle for management over leadership, organization over vision, maintenance over mission. But that's not true leadership. For a business or church to grow, mere maintenance is not an option.

So How Do I Get Started?

Pray. This is a great place to start. Go back to the first quality, which is spirituality. I believe that a God who goes to the trouble to give you gifts will be faithful to help you discover them. Get involved in serving, and see what He blesses. Meet with the divine CEO and ask Him to bring to your mind an honest assessment of your strengths and weaknesses. He will help you to discern your spiritual gifts, natural abilities, and passions.

Read. One book I've enjoyed and recommend is *Now, Discover Your Strengths,*[4] an excellent tool especially for business leaders. *Discovering your Natural Talents*[5] by John Bradley and Jay Carty is another winner. Also, read and study what the Bible says about spiritual gifts, especially in 1 Corinthians 12 and Romans 12.

Ask. Talk to at least 10 to 12 people who have worked with you and ask them, "What value have I added to your life? What is it you most appreciate about me that causes you to give me your business, to serve with me, or to allow me to serve you?" Ask several clients, customers, friends, or members of your church. If you listen well and assess what you hear, you'll begin to discern your unique abilities.

Do. Get busy leading and see what happens! My dad used to say, "It's always easier to steer a moving car." As you step up and lead with a servant's heart, God will begin to show you where you are gifted. Your passions will begin to surface. Your experience base will expand. Life alone will make sure of that! Then focus as much as possible on what God seems to be blessing.

Reflect. At least once a year, spend some time alone to really think about your gifts, passions, and experiences. Write them down and pray about them. Ask God to show you a little more about your true self as a divinely shaped child of God. Then focus as much as possible on making the most of what you've learned about yourself.

Adjust. Every so often, perhaps twice a year, keep off-loading what you don't enjoy or aren't gifted to do and give those tasks to people with a passion for that part of the mission. Keep shifting more and more of your time and energy toward your zone of unique abilities. Never forget this is a lifelong process of discovery, not an instant revelation. Remember:

You are the book you are trying to read,
and new pages are being added every day of your life.

So keep reading. Keep learning. Keep adjusting, day by day, month by month, year by year, moving more of your time and energy toward the center of your target. Less is really more. Specialize to lead...and have a life!

LESS IS MORE Leadership:
Putting *Specialization—the Power of Unique Abilities* into Action

1. Prayerfullycomplete the following:

   My primary gift(s) or abilities are...

   My greatest passion is for serving in...

   A life experience that has shaped me is...

2. Based on what God has shown you concerning your gifts, passions, and experiences, what do you think is your unique *ability?*

3. If you're not sure, what do you think has the *greatest potential* to develop into a unique ability?

4. What one thing could you do this year to explore and develop your gifts and passions for the good of others and the glory of God?

5. What should you "off-load" to free up time for using your unique abilities?

"New wine must be put into fresh wineskins.
And no one, after drinking old wine wishes for new;
for he says, 'The old is good enough.' "
—JESUS TO RELIGIOUS TRADITIONALISTS (LUKE 5:38-39)

"In the future, the world leaders in innovation and creativity
will also be the leaders in everything else."[1]
—DR. HAROLD R. MCALINDON, PRESIDENT,
CAMBRIDGE PHILOSOPHY INSTITUTE

"And failure waits for all who stay
with some success, made yesterday."[2]
—COACH JOHN WOODEN (UCLA)

"Toto, we're not in Kansas anymore."
—DOROTHY, THE WIZARD OF OZ

"Containers contain....
We must risk to leave our containers-turned-cages
and find the grace to dance without stepping on toes."[3]
—GORDON MACKENZIE, HALLMARK CARDS

CHAPTER SEVEN

Innovation—
The Power of Creativity

———

Creativity is often met with criticism, even skepticism, when it suggests "I think there's a better way." Mr. Status Quo chairs most boards and usually has a sizable voting block around the table. So when a new idea comes up, or a suggestion for improvement, it's often squelched quickly...and never gets past the boardroom door.

I once received an email that listed some classic examples of great innovations that met with resistance up front. Here are my favorites:

- "This 'telephone' has too many shortcomings to be seriously considered as a means of communication. The device is inherently of no value to us" (internal memo at Western Union, 1876).

- "Heavier-than-air flying machines are impossible" (Lord Kelvin, president, Royal Society, 1895).

- "Stocks have reached what looks like a permanently high plateau" (professor of economics, Yale University, 1920s).

- "I think there is a world market for maybe five computers" (chairman of IBM, 1943).

161

- "We don't like their sound, and guitar music is on the way out" (recording company rejecting the Beatles, 1962).

- "But what is it good for?" (engineer at IBM commenting on the microchip, 1968).

- "There is no reason anyone would want a computer in their home" (president of an electronic equipment company, 1977).

- "640 ought to be enough (memory) for anybody" (Bill Gates, 1981).

To some degree, we all resist change, especially when it doesn't seem to be necessary. After all, if what we have is "good enough," then why take a risk on an unproven, untested, who-knows-if-it-will-even-fly idea? Yet the companies or churches with the greatest impact on people are usually built on new and innovative approaches. The products that not only beat the competition but redefine the game are usually out-of-the-box. And every leader, including this author, has been short-sighted at one time or another.

One example for me is bottled water. In 1986, a friend of mine told me his relatives who lived in the mountains above Santa Cruz, California, were selling their spring water to a bottling company. This new company was planning to sell water to people—right alongside sodas. I quipped without hesitation, *"That* is the *dumbest idea* I've heard in years. There is no way people are going to pay good money to buy what comes out of their faucet for free." Fast-forward to 2004. Dale begins his most recent vacation by going into a store and purchasing an entire case—36 bottles of water for his family. Someone saw a need, took a risk, and an entire industry was born. I've always heard the quickest way to get rich is to invent a "better mousetrap," but I never dreamed someone would come up with "better water." I thought tap water was good enough. "Good enough" is always the enemy of innovation.

How many times have you rushed through a project and, for whatever reason, stopped and told yourself, *That's good enough,* and then left it at that? You knew you could do better, but for lack of time, resources, or motivation, you decided to settle for good instead of better, or better yet—best.

In Luke 5:37-39, Jesus raised this "good enough" issue when He confronted the religious establishment of His day head-on in a parable about wine and wineskins:

> No one puts new wine into old wineskins; otherwise the new wine will burst the skins and it will be spilled out, and the skins will be ruined. But new wine must be put into fresh wineskins. And no one, after drinking old wine wishes for new; or he says, "The old is good enough."

Jesus wasn't talking only about the nature of the first-century religious establishment. He was also addressing the very nature of mankind, people like you and me. Our tendency is to say, "If it's good enough, then I'm satisfied. If I like what *is*, don't bother me with what *could be*." Once we adopt this attitude, we take that which is merely good and quickly stamp it "good enough." Then we say, "Let's go home!"

In his best-selling analysis of the good-to-great corporate success stories, researcher Jim Collins introduced the problem of "good enough" in this way:

> We don't have great schools, principally because we have good schools. We don't have great government, principally because we have good government. Few people attain great lives, in large part because it is just so easy to settle for a good life. The vast majority of companies never become great, precisely because the vast majority become quite good—and that is their main problem.... That good is the enemy of great is not just a business problem. It is a *human* problem.[4]

So you see, the problem of "good enough" is not just an organizational problem faced by churches and corporations...it is a "*human* problem." It affects and infects every venture attempted by human beings. The research of Jim Collins and the ancient wisdom of Jesus Christ agree: Good enough is the enemy of great.

This means the reason there aren't more great churches or great ministries is because there are many good ones. The reason there aren't more great schools and universities is because there's an ample supply of good ones. And at least one reason there aren't more great leaders is because, by the world's standard, good is "good enough."

Now let's be clear on one point: Jesus wasn't knocking the old wine. He wasn't saying that all things old are bad or irrelevant. The problem was not the wine, but the wineskins, which were too brittle to handle new wine. New wine is alive...fermenting, expanding, and forcing the wineskin to change its shape. One of the deadliest creativity-killers faced by businesses and churches alike is "calcified leadership"—leaders who are rigid, unbending, and inflexible. These leaders are guardians of the status quo. They care more about maintaining corporate traditions and methods than moving the mission forward.

The "Hardening Factors"

What is the cause of "old wineskins disease"? Status quo leaders, like the religious establishment who frustrated Jesus, have *too little*

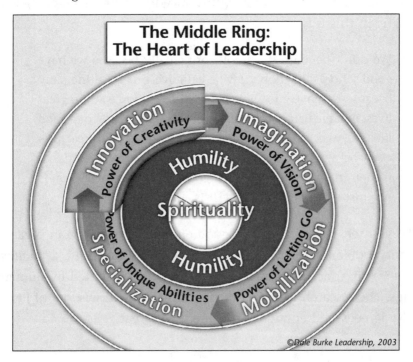

©Dale Burke Leadership, 2003

compassion and *too much contentment*. That's a lethal combination that can bring about mission paralysis and the eventual death of any church or organization. When the leaders become content, then no matter how good the organization is, it has entered the early stages of trouble. And when the company stops caring and loses its compassion for the people it serves, it is headed downward. From there it is just a matter of time before progress grinds to a halt. Organizational death is just around the corner.

When an organization is new, everything is fluid and flexible. Change is the norm. Over time, however, as a company or church adopts more and more policies, procedures, and programs, people start saying, "That's not the way we do it; this is who we are; this is our product; this is how we serve the customer." And eventually, your structures become rigid. Flexible movements, once creative and adaptive, turn into monuments chiseled by past successes.

If any organization is going to stay fresh and alive, then it must learn how to remain soft and flexible like a new wineskin. It's time for an infusion of *innovation*...the power of *creativity*. In today's world, innovation is not just for the entrepreneur, it's for everyone who wants to survive. The future belongs to the leader or organization that learns the art of flexing their forms without forgetting their core values.

If It Ain't Broke...

In the book *If It Ain't Broke...Break It!*, authors Robert Kriegel and Louis Patler tell us that the time to change is when you don't have to. The time to be innovative is when you're on the crest of the wave, not when you're in the trough. I found out about Kriegel and Patler's book from one of my most creative mentors, Dr. Howard Hendricks, the founder of the Center for Christian Leadership in Dallas, Texas. Kriegel and Patler write,

> In the past, change occurred incrementally, at a slower pace. We had the luxury of making long-range projections....But today, the rate of change is accelerating *exponentially*, shifting

so fast it is tough to make even short-term predictions accurately.[5]

John Young, the chairman and CEO of Hewlett Packard, once admitted, "We've become the victims of our own success."[6] Many of the businesses and churches in America have reached a plateau or are in a state of decline for this reason. Every organization, at one point in its history, was growing and successful. The fact is, success is always the first step toward failure. When you think you've reached the top of the hill, you may very well be looking at a descent just ahead. Why? Success tends to shut down our creative juices and bring our innovation to a halt because most of us still follow the "old wineskin" wisdom that says, "If it isn't broken, don't fix it."

> *If God is the ultimate Creator, wouldn't it be a good idea to consult Him when you need a bit of creative genius?*

Instead, as the title of Kriegel and Patler's book says, "If it ain't broke...break it!" By that I don't mean destroy everything now! That's not creative innovation, that's self-destruction. Rather, the real goal for twenty-first-century leaders should be...

To foster a culture of innovation
that encourages and rewards creativity
even when everything seems to be just fine.

Maybe you don't need to "break it," but you better at least "break it down," look it over, and then put it back together...continually! Keep it flexible rather than fixed, always looking for ways to improve your product or better serve your people.

Innovation: Not Just for the Sick and Dying

Ongoing innovation is crucial because the world is always changing. Shortly after taking on my current pastorate, I faced this reality head on. I was following in the footsteps of one of my own heroes, a nationally known and respected leader, Charles Swindoll. Pastor Chuck and his staff had done a great job of growing a strong, healthy church. Yet the church leadership, and I, knew that some changes were needed. There was a new generation of people on the horizon. The church was healthy, but aging. It was cutting-edge in many of its ministries, but there were also real needs that called for change. So I gave a message one evening entitled, "Why Healthy Churches Need Change." The essence of my message was that even healthy churches need innovation because...

"Not only is everything changing, but everything exists in relationship to something else that is changing. If you or your products don't grow, improve and evolve, as in nature, they (and you) will face extinction. Unconventional wisdom says: *Treat your product as if it's alive and it will stay that way.*"[7]

—ROBERT KRIEGEL AND LOUIS PATLER, *IF IT AIN'T BROKE...BREAK IT!*

- our world is constantly changing
- our mission is yet to be accomplished
- our people are constantly changing
- every new generation is a new challenge
- change is easier when you are healthy, not unhealthy
- Scripture gives us our functions, but not our forms
- flexibility should be the norm if we value people over programs
- creativity should always flow from children of the Creator
- the church is a body, a living organism, and a body must change to grow
- every church or ministry has a natural life cycle and will eventually die unless it is "reborn" from within

Every one of those facts of life applies to the business world as well. Every business is ultimately a people business, and people are always changing. In addition, we live and breath in an atmosphere of perpetual change. And as time goes on, this change is accelerating exponentially.

Therefore, the need for innovation can no longer be ignored by anyone hoping to stay in business for the long haul. Yes, leaders have always needed to innovate, but the value of innovation has grown dramatically in the twenty-first century.

Innovation Is Hard Work, But It's Worth It!

Creativity does not come naturally. New ideas, solutions, and approaches to problem-solving require times of solitude and reflection. In short, you need time to think. Margaret Wheatley, who is an author and a consultant in the field of strategic planning, said it well: "Innovation requires thinking and thinking requires time."[8]

The fact that we as leaders need to take time to be creative is affirmed by the fact that it takes more time and energy to solve problems than to create them. So, if we want to get better at anything, it's going to take some time and effort. Becoming more innovative and maximizing your creativity requires the best of you. That's why you need to set aside time to think, reflect, contemplate, and pray. After all, if God is the ultimate Creator, wouldn't it be a good idea to consult Him when you need a bit of creative genius? Attempting to solve problems on the run with your cell phone ringing and the computer dinging to signal that you have mail isn't going to get you where you want to go. You must protect some time to think—time during which you won't be interrupted. Only then will innovation and the power of creativity come to life.

Innovation Stimulators: Four Questions

I want to give you a simple formula for innovative problem solving. This formula will stimulate your thinking and is easy to commit to memory. It includes four questions made up of just eight letters. We can't get any simpler than that!

The four stimulators are:

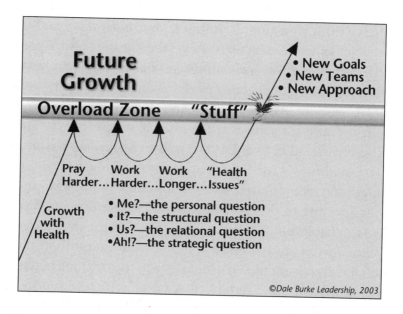

When you explore these four short questions in relation to any problem you or your organization faces, you will be surprised at how many potential solutions and innovations will surface. And if you brainstorm them with a few of your most creative teammates, you may very well end up with results that will exceed your expectations!

The Me? Question: The Personal Issue

The *Me?* question is the personal question. Whenever you're frustrated and you're looking for an innovative solution, always begin with yourself as the leader. With some introspection, you may come to realize you are part of the problem. As a leader, more often than not, when I've asked this question, I've come to discover that my habits, routines, or relationships are preventing me or my church from going to the next level. When that happens, I've got to start with "self-innovation." It's time to change me.

In fact, as you study the LESS IS MORE paradigm, you'll notice it's as much about self-leadership as it is organizational leadership. It's about you, the leader, constantly honing your skills and developing your character as you apply the eight core concepts in this book—your *spirituality*, your *humility*, your *mobilization* of leaders, your *specialization* as you serve from your unique abilities, your *innovation*, and so on. So in a real sense, self-leadership is always the starting point. Changing your own habits, the way you approach your job, and the way you carry out your leadership is one key to making progress. Pray, asking God for His wisdom. Assess yourself, and then change!

A perfect example of this is when I had to adapt to three services at our church instead of two. The fact is, the change had to start with me. No matter how we tried to schedule the morning, it wasn't going to work as long as I required 40 to 45 minutes to present my message. Was I willing to do the hard work of shortening my sermons and change a habit that had become engrained in me over the course of 25 years? I went ahead and gave it a try, and found that the new approach had its advantages! It's forced me to use my time better, and I believe my sermons have improved as a result. And the shorter messages leave people wanting a little more, which is not a bad thing at all. And our people love the change. I guess when it comes to listening to a sermon, maybe less is more after all! Some of the toughest skeptics who questioned the change have even become raving fans.

Now, I'm not recommending 30-minute sermons over 40-minute sermons. If our church had ten more acres of parking that allowed for a quicker turnaround time between our services, I would go back to 40-minute messages. But we don't have that extra parking space, and I have to work within that constraint. I've got to lead in response to reality, not in response to what I wish were the case.

The It? Question: The Structural Issue

The *It?* question is the structural question. A good example of this is what the church leaders did in Acts 6:1-7 with the widows who were not getting enough food. They realized they needed to change the structure: They created a new team of people to handle work they knew would distract them from their main responsibility. They called this new team *deacons*, which comes from a Greek word that means "servants."

Often, churches or companies are structured in ways that inhibit growth. For example, I once talked to another pastor who told me he

⟨⟨⟨⟩⟩⟩

A skeptic turned raving fan...

Dear Dale,

I LOVE the new format. Our Sunday school class is energized—despite being bumped up to Lifestage 5 [note: 5 is the last "Lifestage" in our system]. The services seem too short—it makes you long to come back.... We are having a small group for lunch each week and I would never have felt I could do that on the old schedule.... The music is great and the messages have been wonderful.

I have to admit I felt we didn't need three services and that the third service wouldn't succeed because of the later time and so many of those who might be interested in it already attend our contemporary evening service. Last week I went to this new 11:30 service and I was totally amazed. What a great crowd. What talent there is in that worship team!

I am so glad you are a pastor with vision and an understanding of the needs of the people. I love our church and I am praying for your stamina as you give out so much of yourself.

Thanks for all you do,

Marianne Werschle

didn't have enough time for his sermon preparation. He lamented his heavy load of administration, counseling appointments, and the number of ministry leaders he had to meet with one-on-one. These leaders managed his five most critical ministry teams. I asked him, "Have you considered changing your structure? You're meeting with five different team leaders to check up on how their teams are doing, and that takes a lot of time. Why not create a board and have all five team leaders meet once a month with you? During that meeting, you can have each of them give you an update on their ministries, and then provide them some input to encourage and build them up. That way, you have one meeting instead of five and your leaders will begin to bond as a group and draw on one another for help." This pastor, by simply changing his structure, could better serve his team and restore some valuable time for his "main thing."

The Us? Question: The Relationship Issue

The *Us?* question is the relational or networking question: Who am I spending my time with? People are what empower us. They are our greatest resource. Therefore, we need to be careful about *who* we spend our time with. Many of us develop a close circle of relationships that stays the same for a long time, thus putting ourselves into a relational rut. Creativity is nurtured by meeting new people, building new alliances, and discovering new mentors who can take your leadership or your organization to the next level.

This doesn't mean you should go out and replace your entire network of friends and associates. As a leader, you always need some quality, long-term relationships; a few great friends who share your core values, encourage you, and provide honest accountability. Some of those relationships may very well continue until you leave the planet! But to grow, you must reserve some relational space for people who can stretch you beyond your past. Be wise and careful with your relational time because it's one of your most valuable investment opportunities for the future.

The Ah!? Question: The Strategic Issue

This is when you ask, "Is there one strategic initiative that, if we were to accomplish it, would take us to the next level?" We had to ask ourselves that question at our church when we faced the reality of a changing community demographic. Our congregation was loving, open to all, but still predominantly Caucasian and western European in worship style on Sunday morning. After the last population census, we discovered that our county is now about 48 percent Caucasian and 52 percent "other." So we launched a strategic initiative to offer a new worship service that would be designed for the "52 percent other." Our goal was to better serve the needs of our rapidly growing Hispanic, African-American, and Asian populations in Orange County by offering them a worship environment more in touch with their culture. So we launched a whole new worship venue, lead by a team of gifted new leaders from different ethnic backgrounds. We encouraged them to be innovative and design this worship time to connect with the hearts and souls of the "52 percent." This took a major effort, but it was worth it. Today we have a growing percentage of families from every ethnicity who feel at home in our church, thanks in part to this new, creative worship venue. That's an example of a strategic initiative—which, in turn, stimulates innovation and creativity.

Pioneer or Settler?

How can you create a corporate culture in which innovation is the norm and not the exception? How can you get more of your team to think "outside the box"? As the leader, you often feel the pressure to always be coming up with the next good idea, new product, or creative change that will keep you on the edge. The truth is, you should never tackle the innovation challenge alone. You need to build a culture of creativity that encourages everyone to contribute.

This is not easy to do, because over time, most organizations get settled in their ways to the point of stifling creativity. Virtually all new companies and churches are born with a pioneering, innovative spirit. Then they experience success, and begin to settle down. Their past successes begin to restrain the coming generation of "pioneer leaders." We begin as pioneers, but soon turn into settlers. The cycle looks something like this:

Start...
    succeed...
        standardize...
            settle down...
                stay put...
                    struggle...why?

Ruts, Hairballs, and Ghosts of the Past

Success always leaves a mark on the trail, just like the ruts of a wagon. Initially these ruts make a great guide. The tested trail is always a safer route. So back in pioneer days, when someone found a good path from point A to point B, others would eagerly follow. Over time, the path developed ruts—ruts that served a purpose. They not only showed the way, they helped keep the wagons on course. It was like putting the horses or oxen on cruise control! Yet over time, these ruts got deeper and deeper—until they not only guided the wagons, but they also fought against any driver who dared to try and go another direction. Routines are great to a point, but when a routine becomes a rut, watch out!

Your ruts, the *result* of past successes,
begin to not only *record* where you have been,
they now *control* where you are going!

The power of creativity is unleashed in your organization when everyone on the team has the freedom to explore new paths en route to the agreed-upon destination. If the vision is clear, you can entrust to your people the freedom to pioneer and explore. The *mission* is the key, not the *methods*. It's the destination, not the route, that matters.

Gordon MacKenzie served in the creative production department of Hallmark Cards for 30 years to the day. He excelled and climbed the ladder of creativity and the organization until he was asked to head up the entire team of more than 600 creative designers. His book, *Orbiting the Giant Hairball,* is the story of his struggle to stay connected to a giant organization full of procedures and policies (the "Hairball") and yet maintain his personal creative edge. He became known, officially, as the "Creative Paradox" at Hallmark. He wrote:

> So create I did. But during those 30 years, there was not a day when I was not subject to the inexorable pull of Corporate Gravity tug, tug, tugging me toward (and, during one unhappy year, right into) the tangle of the Hairball, *where the ghosts of past successes outvote original thinking.*[9]

I love the picture he paints: The ghosts of the past still have a vote! MacKenzie's challenge to creative employees, church members, and leaders is to recognize that hairballs are a part of life. Every church or company has a "hairball"—if it has a history, it has its hairball, along with the ghosts who haunt anyone who dares to untangle it! But don't be sucked in by the "gravity" of the corporate history. Instead, learn to "orbit the hairball":

> Orbiting is responsible creativity; vigorously exploring and operating beyond the Hairball of the corporate mind set, beyond "accepted models, patterns, or standards"—all the while remaining connected to the spirit of the corporate mission.[10]

It is the commitment to a common mission and common core values that creates the freedom to "orbit" without flying off into space, disconnected from the organization altogether. Your personal explorations into the world of creativity must not be in pursuit of your own mission, but that of the church or organization. Every leader must stay accountable to the mission. Yes, you can ignore the hairball and fly off into space in pursuit of your own agenda. But beware—there's a word for such space travelers: *unemployed!*

So how do we create a culture of creativity that can overcome the ruts, hairballs, and ghosts of our past successes?

Seven Tips for Creating a Culture of Creativity

1. Emphasize Mission over Method

Jesus, in His final words to His followers, continually reinforced the mission, the mission, and mission:

> "Go therefore and make disciples of all the nations" (Matthew 28:19).

> "You shall be My witnesses...even to the remotest part of the earth" (Acts 1:8).

> "Shepherd My sheep" (John 21:16).

As a leader, you need to constantly remind your people that methods and forms should never direct us. They are not why you are in business. You need to keep pointing your team back to the organization's mission. I tell our church often that our message and mission are fixed; they *will not change*. But our methods must always remain flexible if we want to enjoy a long life.

Even if your business is built on a product, don't let the product become your obsession. The more you can think beyond the product to the value it provides your customers, the more you'll stay focused on your mission. I recently attended a leadership seminar led by Warren Bennis, who had just spent the day with Howard Shultz, the founder of Starbucks. Shultz credited the success of Starbucks to this mission focus:

> We are not in the coffee business serving people.
> We are in the people business serving coffee.[11]

No matter what your business, as a leader following the premier mentor, Jesus Christ, you should always remember His advice:

> It's always about serving others.
> To be great, be a servant.

While on a trip to speak on leadership to a group of my peers, I came across a fascinating article in *USA Today* on one of the major film-making companies. The article raised a vitally important question: How does a film company plan to stay in business when the indicators are that its product may soon become totally obsolete as the world goes digital? Now the company's *method* was centered on the manufacture and development of photographic film; but that wasn't their real *mission*. They haven't really been in the *film* business at all, but in the *imaging* business. The recording, transferring, and reproduction of images was their real business. Yet even behind this process was a deeper purpose: They were in the business of recording memories for people. That was their real mission!

As long as this company focuses on their real business, the underlying value they provide to their customer, they won't feel threatened by today's trend toward digital photography. Instead, they will get creative and adapt so they can stay in the game. Capturing images is no longer the sole domain of cameras and film. The world is fast going digital. Even my kids' cell phones (we adults are always two generations behind our kids) can now snap a picture and transfer it instantly across the country, at no extra cost!

So, whatever business you're in, keep your focus and your team's focus on the real mission—not the methods. As a result, you will nurture a more innovative culture.

2. Assess Regularly with a Servant Spirit

Assess your product and your service regularly. Never stop asking, "How can we better serve your needs?" Study the trends your customers are following. Talk with those who are leaving or no longer using your service. Listen with a humble, servant attitude. Don't ever fall into the rut of thinking, *This must be good enough.* Your customers may help you discover the next "better trail" over the mountains!

Earlier, we learned that humility empowers and improves every aspect of our leadership. I believe humility empowers innovation because it prompts you to constantly ask your customers, your congregation, even your community, "What do you think?" They may have suggestions that will trigger your next breakthrough idea. So ask, and then listen, listen, listen...and learn.

3. Create Time Just to Think

As I mentioned earlier, significant "think time" allows creative seeds to germinate. In the next chapter we will look at how we can organize our week, month, and year to provide for and then protect quality time for reflection and innovative thought. Yet allow me to briefly emphasize the importance of regular time for reassessing and refocusing your life. In the routine of your week you need four kinds of quality time...which will help you become a better leader:

⟨⟨⟨⟩⟩⟩

Gomer Pyle Is *Not* Your Customer

"It didn't matter what life handed Gomer Pyle, USMC—he just rolled with the punches. Good surprises. Bad surprises. No worries. Gomer would spread his smile from cheek to cheek, turn his head side to side and crow, 'Su-PRIZE, Su-PRIZE, Su-PRIZE.' Gomer LOVED surprises.

"But Gomer Pyle was a TV character. Real people, the people who interact with your organization, don't typically care for last-minute changes, adjustments, revisions, or anything else that even sounds like a Su-PRIZE.

"I started thinking about this after reading a report on the reason online shoppers give for abandoning their shopping cart near the end of a transaction. According to NetIQ, 35 percent of the carts are left standing in their virtual aisle when shoppers are surprised by what they find on the shipping and delivery time pages. You have probably done this yourself—especially with websites that don't reveal an item is out of stock until the very end of the transaction. I have tried to avoid sites that don't show stocking levels up front.

"Many times we catch our customers off guard because we assume they know the intricacies of our business....Unannounced changes in price, product design, packaging quantities and even new office hours can be frustrating to customers—especially long-term customers who have come to rely on us to do things a certain way.

"Of course, last-minute changes are inevitable and—as customers—we need to give our vendors a certain amount of grace when they happen. The challenge lies in trying to eliminate the 'systematic surprises' that occur so often you begin to believe the organization has 'surprise' as one of its core values....

"One of the hardest things to do is to look at your organization from a customer's perspective. To eliminate unwanted surprises you are best advised to lace up a pair of THEIR shoes and walk a mile or two."[12]

—Jim Seybert
Brainstorm and Ideation Consultant

Rest time—This is quality rest time for the refreshment and restoration of your body, soul, and mind. I call this "Sabbath rest" in the next chapter. Quality think time is a vital component of Sabbath rest. It allows you to set your mind on the voice, vision, and values of God that anchor your personal life and your relationship with God and your family.

Results time—By this I mean blocks of undistracted time during which you can concentrate on your "main thing." This is time for those few things that are mission critical, top priority, or flow from your unique abilities. Quality think time is a part of producing great results.

Response time—These blocks of time are dedicated to the needs of others. All of us, as servant leaders, ought to be prepared and able to respond in a timely fashion to the real needs of members on our team.

Refocus time—Set aside some half or full days for assessing, evaluating, and adjusting your plan for your rest, results, and response. Refocus time is your prime time for reviewing your objectives and priorities. Quality think time is an essential part of refocusing.

4. Brainstorm Together with a Creative Team

Pull together a small group of your most creative people and brainstorm together. As you do, adopt a "no idea is out of bounds" rule. Resist the temptation to evaluate ideas as they flow from the group. There will be time later to throw out what doesn't work. For a while, just flood the room with ideas!

In this kind of setting, the team will move into interactive innovation and feed off each other's creativity. The leader who thinks he or she must solve all the problems alone will never maximize his or her potential. Set aside some blocks of time, get your idea people together, and watch the creative power of the group take you to places you would've never gone alone!

For example, when I work on a sermon series, I always do the message preparation alone. But when it comes time to title the series or the sermons, I bring together two or three creative staff members to help me. I tell them, "This is the raw content of what I'll be communicating. Can you help me come up with the title, the hook?" When we start brainstorming, we don't care how wacky the title is—no title is bad because the purpose is to brainstorm without critiquing. It's important to fill the air with ideas first, not shoot them down before they even get their chance to land!

Dr. Howard Hendricks, one of the most creative and innovative leaders alive today, taught me, "If you want to come up with a great title for anything, first come up with 50 possibilities. Resist the tendency to critique them. Then go back and refine the best of the list. That's how you get a winner."

5. Allow Risk, Failure, and the Freedom to Experiment

In general, our education system in America punishes innovation and devalues experimentation. Students, from very early on, are taught to "color inside the lines." And they get graded down if they go outside the boundaries (in legitimate ways, of course).

Remember, you will become what you celebrate....so celebrate "rebirth-days"!

Gordon MacKenzie, the creative leader at Hallmark, likes to put it this way: "containers contain." That's a simple but often overlooked truth. The fact is, our forms *serve* us but also *shape* us. They carry the message, but they can also constrict the messenger if we are not careful. We must create an environment that allows innovators to "color outside the lines." Otherwise, your people will be afraid to venture too far from the norm or from the security of last year's ruts. MacKenzie wrote,

> If we are to achieve the quantum leaps the future seems to be demanding of us, we must risk to leave our containers-turned-cages and find the grace to dance without stepping on toes.[13]

Allowing failure is absolutely essential if we're going to come up with breakthrough ideas. Get over the fear of failure. If you've had no failures, that may be a sign there's little or no innovation taking place. If you think an idea might have good potential but you or others feel it's a little too scary or risky, then label the venture an experiment. This will help put everyone's fears at ease. More than once in the past I've told fellow staff members or the congregation, "Look, we're going to try this for three months, and if it doesn't work, we don't have to stay with it." By granting the freedom to experiment, you encourage innovation while lowering fear.

6. Celebrate and Reward Your Innovators

Over time, an organization will become what it celebrates. If you celebrate your past and talk only about your history, you will empower the ghosts of the past. But if you honor and celebrate your pioneers, you will foster a pioneering culture. Be public with your praise for those who color outside the lines, as long as they are "adding color" while staying true to the values and vision of the group and drawing within the boundaries of God's Word and the mission.

This is especially important when a team risks and struggles or fails. Even then, you can celebrate their courage and willingness to risk. You always have employees or members who are sitting on good ideas but are afraid to bring them up because they think, *If I try this and it doesn't work, then I'm out of a job.* Or, *I'm going to be laughed at or ridiculed.* You need to look for opportunities to celebrate the people who share their innovative ideas if you want to tap their full creativity.

One of the greatest ways to do this is through storytelling. Tell the stories of new, exciting attempts to change lives, advance the mission, and be all that God has called you to be. This can be done through newsletter articles, letters to members, announcements, updates, and testimonies. This doesn't mean you should ignore your history or past achievements. Today's pioneers depend upon the resources provided by past successes. So it's okay to visit and honor your past as testimony to God's faithfulness over the years; just don't settle down there. Keep a balance between celebrating the past and innovation. Remember, you will become what you celebrate. So don't just celebrate birthdays—celebrate "rebirth-days"!

7. Watch, Listen, and Learn from Others

Watch, listen, and learn from others both in and outside of your own team. This is yet another affirmation of how humility in leadership actually empowers more effective innovation. The prideful leader thinks he or she already has it figured out. Pride says, "We're the best, so why look and learn from others?" That's a sure way to kill creativity.

I once read an article about a company that stimulated innovation by bringing problems to a department that had no experience or direct interest in that particular issue. For example, if they wanted to stimulate sales of a product, they would go to the engineering department and ask them to brainstorm sales ideas. Or if they had an engineering problem, they would invite marketing staff to brainstorm possible solutions. Lo and behold, the group with no engineering expertise would see a solution the engineers were blind to see. That's because their "engineering glasses" hampered their creative vision.

We all tend to get locked into our own box and our own way of approaching problems. That's why it's helpful to go outside of your "normal" circle of contacts in search of innovative approaches. Sometimes the best solutions are very simple ideas you've been overlooking all along. That's one reason that I, as a pastor, love to network with business leaders. I learn a lot when I run my vision and values through a marketplace grid because I often discover business ideas that can be adapted to help me become a more effective pastor. Good leadership principles are usually effective in a variety of settings, so learn from one another. Start by running every idea through the filter of God and His Word, then adapt the best of the best ideas to your mission.

Innovate, But Beware...

I have a seminar for leaders that I've titled, "Innovation: How to Do Ministry on the Edge Without Falling Off the Cliff." Allow me to close this chapter with a warning from that seminar: There *is* a cliff. It is possible to go too far as you innovate to connect with your world. Whether you are building a business or growing a church, be sure to anchor yourself in the first discipline, spirituality. Remember the priority of the voice, vision, and values of God and His kingdom.

And in regard to vision, remember this:

The best change happens
when you first decide what should never change.

Guard your core vision and values with a passion. Keep listening to the voice of the one Master, the ultimate CEO of your life and leadership. When I train pastors to lead, I remind them that an estimated 80 percent of all churches in America are on a plateau or declining. Why? For one of *two* reasons:

Some churches die because they change
what they should *never* change;
while other churches die because they *refuse* to change
what they are *free* to change.

In the church, we should never change our message or our mission. If we do, we will no longer have a message worth sharing. God's Word and the good news of Jesus Christ will never go out of style. Never abandon the message or mission in the name of innovation. But other churches die for the second reason—because they refuse to change what they are free to change. If we refuse to flex our methods, we may find ourselves with a message...but no audience. The same is true for every leader, whether in ministry or in the marketplace. There are some things we should never change, no matter what our culture thinks or says or demands. There are other things we should be willing to change without batting an eye! How can we know the difference?

Anchor yourself in God's eternal Truth—His vision and values—and you'll be ready to sail with whatever winds blow your way. This may sound like a contradiction—"get anchored so you can set sail"—yet it is wisdom. Slow down and remember your core values, and you'll be ready to launch. Listen to the One who does not change, and then you'll have a word or message of eternal relevance to share.

Firm up what you will never give up,
and then flex as God leads on everything else.

Summed up, listening to the Creator is the first step toward asking, "What if?" and unleashing your God-given creativity. *Then* you can innovate!

LESS IS MORE Leadership:
Putting *Innovation—the Power of Creativity* into Action

1. List one challenge or obstacle you or your ministry/organization currently face:

2. Now ask and answer the four questions for innovators: Me? It? Us? and Ah!?

3. List any ideas you have for innovation or change in these areas:

    What *personal habits* can help you move forward?

    Your *structures*...do they inhibit you or allow for change?

    Your *relationships* or networks...which ones help you advance the mission? Resource you? Or stimulate your creativity?

    What *strategic move* could you explore that has *breakthrough* potential to move you forward?

4. What will you do this year to encourage a culture of creativity and innovation?

The Outer Ring:
The Heart of Execution

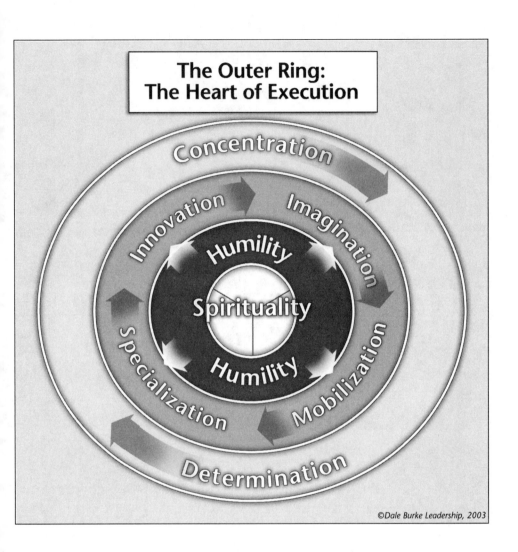

The Outer Ring:
The Heart of Execution

Concentration

Innovation

Imagination

Humility

Spirituality

Humility

Specialization

Mobilization

Determination

©Dale Burke Leadership, 2003

The Outer Ring:
The Heart of Execution

This now brings us to the third and final ring of LESS IS MORE Leadership—the outer ring, which is labeled "The Heart of Execution." This is where the visionary leader encounters the resistance of the world as he tries to live out his plan for leading and living as God designed. This is where the proverbial rubber meets the road. He will need healthy routines of execution. The disciplines of the outer ring allow the leader…

<blockquote>
to be disappointed yet not derailed;
to handle distractions while remaining on task;
to protect the important from the urgent;
to balance his serving and leading;
to protect time for rest as well as results,
for responding to needs, and getting refocused;
and no matter what, to never lose hope.
</blockquote>

Every church, company, or organization has built-in inertia that must be overcome if progress is to be made or momentum maintained.

The disciplines of the outer ring are essential to implementing and maintaining effective leadership with a balanced life.

This ring consists of two disciplines, *concentration* and *determination*. These help the leader to unleash the concentrated *power of focus* and the sustaining *power of hope*. In short, this ring unfolds a practical plan for getting the job done—*execution*.

"Therefore I run in such a way, as not without aim;
I box in such a way, as not beating the air."
—APOSTLE PAUL ON FOCUS (1 CORINTHIANS 9:26)

"The eagle that chases two rabbits at one time
will catch neither."
—ANCIENT CHINESE PROVERB

When asked what was the most important shot in golf:
"The next one."
—BEN HOGAN, GOLF LEGEND

"Effective Executives...do not start with their tasks.
They start with their time."[1]
PETER DRUCKER, *THE EFFECTIVE EXECUTIVE*

"In the early morning, while it was still dark,
Jesus got up, left the house, and went away to a secluded place,
and was praying there....they found Him, and said to Him,
'Everyone is looking for you.'
He said to them, 'Let us go somewhere else...
that I may preach there also;
for that is what I came for.' "
—JESUS ON FOCUS (MARK 1:35-38)

CHAPTER EIGHT

Concentration—
The Power of Focus

A<small>S</small> we slipped into the booth for lunch, the young pastor of a growing ministry opened up and dumped his frustration. "I don't know what's wrong with me. I'm not only busy, I'm buried by all the stuff of ministry all week long. I went into ministry to teach the Word—that's my passion. But some weeks I'm not getting to my sermon prep until Friday, or even Saturday! And I never seem to have time to plan ahead, meet with my key leaders, let alone envision our next steps to move us forward."

This young leader was experiencing what I call the "downside of success." As we learned earlier, success can kill a leader, an organization, or both. Growth in any enterprise brings with it new demands and pressures. God was blessing this man's efforts, without a doubt. However, the look on his face was one of frustration, not fulfillment. He felt like the proverbial hamster on the wheel, running faster, harder, and longer, only to step out of the wheel and discover the scenery had not changed one bit. And his "cage" was filling up with even more "stuff" than ever!

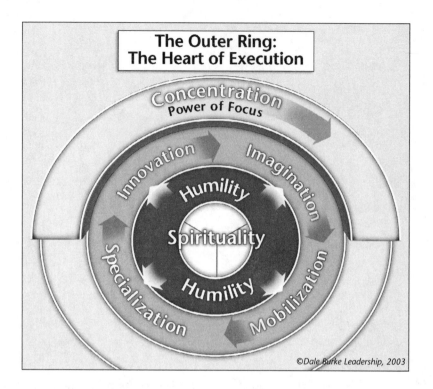

The young man was also concerned about the impact on his family. He and his wife were committed to ministry, but the routine was growing old. He began to wonder, *Would this continue for the rest of their lives? Would it get even worse as the ministry grew? Would they be able to develop a routine or find a way to juggle the demands of ministry and family so that both stayed healthy, grew, and remained fun?* In short, he was asking, "Can I lead and still have a life?"

I knew exactly how he felt. I have been in that "cage" many times during my 25 years as a pastor. And as I've taught the LESS IS MORE Leadership seminars around the country, I've discovered that this state of working from "under the pile" is not the exception but the norm for most pastors or leaders in any field. In fact, it is the frustrating reality of many leaders who experience the "blessing" of success. Success, oddly enough, can become your number-one enemy unless you learn to adjust to the growing demands on your time. Most leaders respond by praying harder, working harder, and staying longer hours to get it all done. But that just doesn't solve the problem. Besides, God is not in the business of using and abusing His leaders, burning them out so He can pick up another young one every ten years. God's will is for healthy servant-leaders to lead healthy businesses or ministries until they check out for heaven.

Juggling—a Fact of Life

The need to learn to juggle various demands is a fact of leadership. Every leader, whether in ministry or the marketplace, must learn the art of juggling. The dream of juggling only one ball will never become a reality, unless that one ball is unemployment! And even then, the demands of life are numerous. The secret is not juggling as fast as you can, but rather, learning how to juggle more effectively and selectively.

First, recognize that even the best of jugglers begin by choosing what they are going to juggle. They may juggle balls, pins, razor-sharp knives, or flaming batons, but they never juggle a diverse collection of everything anyone can throw their way. I believe the demands of leadership are best juggled *one type at a time.*[2] Every healthy leader must learn to juggle the four "R's," or the four major types of time or activities. All four are essential if the leader desires to grow to his maximum potential and still experience real joy: Rest, Results, Response,

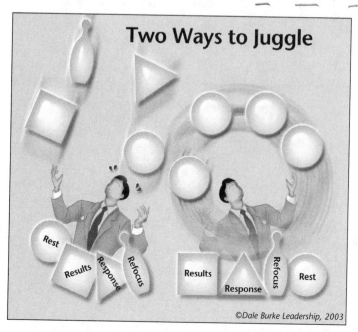

Two Ways to Juggle

Rest
Results
Response
Refocus

Results
Response
Refocus
Rest

©Dale Burke Leadership, 2003

and Refocus. Let's look now at how this breakdown can help us master concentration, or the power of focus.

The Four Types of Time

All leadership activity can be categorized into the four types of time. Learning to sort all you do into these four categories will help you juggle your demands effectively, spend less time picking up dropped balls, and even enjoy a regular day of no juggling at all! Here are the four categories:

- **Rest Time**   *Focusing on your health, your spirituality, and marriage*
- **Results Time**   *Focusing on the "main things" that advance the mission*
- **Response Time** *Focusing on cleaning up and following up your "stuff"*
- **Refocus Time**   *Focusing on and adjusting what and how you should juggle*

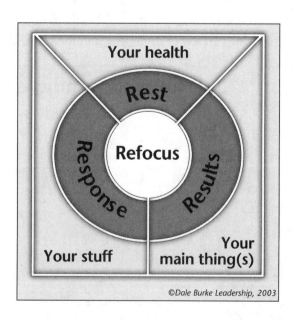

©Dale Burke Leadership, 2003

Thinking of your work in these terms will enable you to be a servant-leader who is available to people, and will protect the time you need for your main priorities related to the inner and middle rings of leadership. It will allow ample time for the four-fold cycle of visionary leadership, so you can focus on...

>**imagination**—the power of *vision*,
>>**mobilization**—the power of *letting go*, entrusting leadership to others,
>>>**specialization**—the power of serving from your *unique abilities*, and
>>>>**innovation**—the power of *creativity*.

It will also allow you to relax and enjoy some "Sabbath rest" every week with your family. Yes, it can be done! These days "off" are essential for the leader who wants to really be "on" during the week. Since spirituality is at the core or heart of the leader, this time of rest must not be labeled as optional. Balance *is possible,* no matter how many times you've tried and failed. There *is a better way* to juggle, and juggle well. Let's get started by laying some foundational guidelines:

First, plan your week in larger chunks of time, preferably full or half days. When a juggler gets in the groove, he stays there for awhile. He concentrates and gets his rhythm going until the process flows naturally. He would never think of taking a phone call or checking his email while flipping sharp knives over his head! Leaders need to learn to focus on one objective at a time and allow enough time to do it well.

I've separated my week into larger blocks of time, full or half-day units, devoted to either *rest, results, response,* or *refocus* activities. Every week, you need some significant blocks of time fully devoted to the first three activities and then periodically, to the fourth. It's not that you can't do individual tasks in minutes or hours. The key is to arrange your week in terms of the four kinds of time or activities, which enables you to tackle related activities together—just like juggling one type of item at a time.

Second, don't mix the objectives. When you *rest,* really, truly rest. Most of us have *to work at not working! Do not carry work into your world of rest or you will pollute its purity and dilute its impact.* When you're in your *results* mode, focus on your mission. Don't let distractions intrude into these times dedicated to your "main thing." When you're in your *response time*, give yourself away as a humble servant. Don't keep looking over your shoulder at the pile of unfinished business waiting for you. Enjoy having some time to just be available to people, to respond to your teammates, and serve. And when you get away to *refocus*, allow yourself plenty of time to listen to God, reflect, and rethink how you want to approach the coming week, month, or year. But during your *refocus time*, leave the cell phone at home, or at least out of sight!

Third, do one thing at a time. How important is it for us to learn to carry out one objective at a time? There's a story told by Peter Drucker, a legend in the field of management, of one of the most accomplished time managers he ever met. This president of a large bank impressed Drucker with both his focus and efficiency. The president would meet with Drucker once a month for 90 minutes, but would always have *only one item* on the agenda. Drucker observed:

> During the hour and a half I was in his office every month, there was never a telephone call, and his secretary never stuck her head in the door to announce that an important man wanted to see him urgently. One day I asked him about this. He said, "My secretary has strict instructions not to put anyone through except the President of the United States and my wife. The president rarely calls—and my wife knows better. Everything else the secretary holds till I have finished. Then I have half an hour in which I return every call and make sure I get every message. I have yet to come across a crisis which could not wait ninety minutes."[3]

The secret here is "one thing at a time." On my desk is a plaque with an ancient Chinese proverb that reads, "The eagle that chases two rabbits at one time will catch neither." A single focus is critical to top performance in anything we do. So during your workday, start with one of the four types of time, and then focus on one activity at a time. Test this, and see if it doesn't dramatically increase both the quality and the quantity of your output.

And ultimately, it's up to us to create that low-distraction environment that fosters a singular focus. The four "R's"—*rest time, results time, response time,* and *refocus time*—each deserve your full attention. A leader who regularly gives focused attention to all four kinds of time in separate blocks will be able to live in balance, stay healthy, and increase his or her productivity. You can lead and still have a life. It starts by focusing on less, not more, in order to get more accomplished. Less is more.

When I try to juggle these four kinds of activity, or even two, into one block of time, I experience frustration and defeat. My stress goes up and my productivity goes down. I'm like the juggler who tries to handle a ball, a knife, and a flaming baton all at once. Or worse yet, like the juggler who tries to handle whatever the audience throws at him! Yet that is exactly what many pastors I consult with are trying to do. They allow others to pass them anything at any time and then struggle to keep all the balls, batons, and knives in the air at one time. On top of all this activity they are expected to listen to God during the week and come to church on Sunday with a fresh word from heaven. It is an impossible task! And of course, even for those who are not pastors, leadership takes concentration, and that means doing one thing at a time.

Let's take a closer look now at the four kinds of time and activity, and see how we can put them into action.

Rest Time

Rest time is when you focus on your health—especially on your spiritual life, marriage, and family. This is not a new idea but an ancient one from Scripture. God designed all His creation to observe a day of rest, and He commanded that we set aside one day per week for rest. I recommend we use this day of rest for refreshment and reinforcement of our spirituality, which includes taking care of our vital relationships, such as marriage, family, or friends. God established this command early on, right in the beginning of the Bible:

By the seventh day God completed His work which He had done,
and He rested on the seventh day from all his work....
Then God blessed the seventh day and sanctified it (Genesis 2:2-3).

Remember the sabbath day, to keep it holy.
Six days you shall labor and do all your work,
but the seventh day is a sabbath of the LORD your God;
in it you shall not do any work... (Exodus 20:8-9).

> ⟨⟨⟨⟩⟩⟩
>
> "It has been proven that leaders who block time working through their roles, goals and their action steps each month, live more intentionally. After spending time monthly listening to God, they develop a sense of confidence and clarity."
>
> —TIM CAHILL, CEO, SOUTH PACIFIC FINANCIAL CORPORATION

You, like the rest of creation, are actually healthier and more productive when you don't work 24/7, as our culture often demands. In some faiths, this day begins at sundown on Friday. Others emphasize Saturday as the original Sabbath, while most Christians use Sunday as their day for rest and worship. My concern is not exactly *when* we do it, but *that* we do it! Very few people in today's busy culture, especially leaders, take the time to have a true, 24-hour day of rest.

I was at a meeting once with a highly respected Christian business leader, and the topic of taking a full day of rest each week came up. He had been challenged by a corporate mentor to rest one day a week and do no work. When he pushed a little to see if his friend really meant "no work," he was surprised. His corporate coach urged him to hold tight to the standard of no work at all—no phone calls, no business-related journals, no quick check-in with the office, not even a work-related email—for a 24-hour period.

The truth is, we're not listening to God or serving Him... if we don't rest.

The executive told us, "By that definition, I realized I had not taken a single day of rest in the last twenty years!" He made a commitment to begin practicing this discipline, and declared that it had refreshed his life and improved his output at work. He challenged us—a room full of busy, megachurch pastors—to do the same. He also exhorted us to begin teaching our congregations the importance and value of a full day of rest.

Pastors and other Christian leaders are some of the worst violators of this divine principle for a healthy life. We excuse ourselves by saying, "We're serving God. We don't have time to rest!" However, the truth is, we're not listening to God, or serving Him as He prescribed, if we don't rest. The Boss has clearly said we're to slow down and take a day off. So if you don't take one day a week to rest, are you in or out of the will of God? The answer is all too obvious and convicting for most of us. Creation always runs better and smoother when it operates by God's design, and you are part of God's creation. As we learned back in chapter 1, we are an "omni-nothing," a limited resource. And God's design for all who serve under His leadership is, "Go for six, but then take a break."

God still loves us in spite of our busyness, but He must get frustrated about our work habits. I can imagine Him saying, "Can't they read? I mean, I put this early on in the Book. I even made it part of the top-ten list to Moses so they wouldn't miss it." He must shake His head and frown as we "sacrifice" our day off for Him, and then have the nerve to complain about our workload.

In Mark 1:35, Jesus modeled for us the priority of rest. After one of the busiest days of His life, caring for people, healing people, and with the "whole city" gathered wanting one more miracle from Him (Mark 1:33), He slipped away, by Himself. He got alone, connected with His Father and prayed. He didn't try to keep up the hectic pace. He knew it was time to clock out. If Jesus, as the Son of God, needed time alone with His Father to refocus and refresh His spirit, how much more must we need the same! If you want to be able to run fast, you must first slow down, stop, and get some rest. Less really is more.

My intent isn't to be legalistic about getting rest, but to make you stop and think. I recognize that we as Christian leaders do not live under Old Testament law. Yet the principle of rest predates even the law. Like gravity, it affects all of creation and has an effect on you whether you believe it or not. My challenge to leaders is to go ahead and try it—do no work for one day, absolutely nothing, and see if you aren't more refreshed by the experience and more effective in the days that follow. I myself have found that taking Mondays as a day of rest for me and my wife has done more to keep me sane and happy under the pressure of ministry than any other single routine in my life.

Results Time

For results time, I recommend you set aside several half-day or full-day blocks of time to focus on your "main things." Results time is driven by the *mission*, and your *unique role* in moving it forward. Again, Jesus is a great role model. In Mark 1:35-37, right after Jesus slipped away to rest and reconnect with His heavenly Father, His leadership team tracked Him down and expressed with apparent disgust, "Everyone is looking for you" (verse 37). In other words, "Boss, the customers are lining up, the phones are lighting up, and the in-box is piling up with emails from hurting people wanting your touch. Let's hurry up and get back to work." Yet Jesus headed a new direction. He walked away from the people who were pursuing Him. At least for now, their needs would have to go unmet. He calmly redirected the team, "Let us go somewhere else...that I may preach there also; for that is what I came for" (Mark 1:38).

Jesus refused to let other people set His agenda. As a leader, He got away, rested and refocused, and then resumed what was indeed mission critical. His mission took priority, even over the real needs of some real people who really wanted His touch. He loved people. He cared about them and their hurts. Yet He knew how to focus and protect prime time for accomplishing His main thing. He was not first and foremost a healer of broken people, but rather, He had a message to get out—a message He knew would

> ❮❮❰❱❯❯
>
> "Without rest time, I cannot focus, and then I'm frustrated and work harder, and then I'm more tired—and it is a vicious cycle."
>
> —GARY JOHNSON, CORPORATE SAFETY DIRECTOR, 40 YEARS IN MANAGEMENT AT LARGE CORPORATIONS, INCLUDING XEROX

ultimately heal millions. Jesus would again set aside time to simply give Himself away to the needs of the masses. (That's what I call *response* time.) But after serving their needs, He was always careful to return to His main thing—His mission. What a great picture of how to handle this tension faced by every servant-leader! There will come times when you must set aside the urgent in order to return to the truly important.

Now in order to make the most of your results time, you must first define what your main things are. Here's my definition:

My **main things** are activities that are
mission-critical, top priority, or
grow out of my unique abilities.

Mission Critical

All of us have something (or a few things) that need to be done well if we want the mission to move forward. They are *mission critical*—they are essential to the health and growth of the business or ministry. This main thing (or things) may change, at least to some degree, as your organization grows. If you are part of a team, then changes in your job description will alter your main things. Mission critical issues may have to become part of your main thing, even if they don't line up with your passions or experiences. That is leadership in the real world. Yet over time, you want to redirect your focus, as much as possible, back into tasks that fully utilize the gifts, passions, and experiences God has given you.

Unique Abilities

Every leader is under construction and never completed as long as life goes on. Therefore, your main things should stay as flexible as your job allows. Let it be redefined from year to year as your unique abilities—gifts, passions, and experiences—develop or expand. Every leader, and every person in the organization, should strive to keep growing and learning, especially about themselves. Encourage personal discovery and then do your best to redirect everyone on your team toward full utilization of their unique gift-passion-experience mix.

Top Priority

Every person, from the corporate CEO to the church volunteer, should clearly understand what he or she is expected to accomplish. What needs to get done? Then, of all their responsibilities, which one, two, or three sit at the top of the list? These now become the top priorities for my *results time*. Many leaders know their long list, the total scope of their responsibilities. But many give me a blank stare when I ask for the short list, the one-to-three top-priority items that trump everything else. Learning to focus on your priorities one at a time is a critical leadership concept.

Around 100 years ago, Charles Schwab, president of Bethlehem Steel, wanted to help himself and his key managers become more efficient. Ivy Lee, a management expert, told Schwab he could increase their efficiency and sales in just one 15-minute session with each executive. Schwab asked him how much it would cost and Ivy replied, "Nothing for now. But after three months, send me a check for what you think it was worth." Lee Ivy gave each one the following advice:

> Write down the most important things you have to do tomorrow. Now, number them in the order of their true importance. The first thing tomorrow morning, start working on item Number 1, and stay with it until completed. Then take item Number 2 the same way. Then Number 3, and so on. Don't worry if you don't complete everything on the schedule. At least you will have completed the most important projects before getting to the less-important ones.[4]

After three months Schwab studied the results, and sent Ivy Lee a check for $25,000. At the time, the average annual salary for an attorney or similar professional was about $2,000 to $3,000 a year. So Schwab valued the advice to be worth about 12 years of full-time attorney fees—by today's wages, well over $1 million! This is literally million-dollar advice for any leader willing to take it seriously.

As leaders, we need to carefully choose what really needs to get done, and then focus on those tasks one thing at a time without distraction. As you plan your results time, remember the following.

Leadership Tip:

Determine your main things,

set your priorities,

tackle them one at a time,

and use the best part of your day.

So, be absolutely clear on your main thing and set aside your best, most productive time of the day or week to carry out those vital tasks. Apart from an occasional crisis, there really is no excuse for pushing your main things to the back burner.

My number one main thing is my weekly teaching of the Scriptures. It is a core value of our church and mission critical to all we do. So I jealously guard most of my Wednesday, every Thursday morning, and every Friday morning for prayer, study, and prep time. I normally study at home, free of office distractions, in order to focus solely on this one vital task. By doing so, I have increased my efficiency and effectiveness dramatically. Time with my leadership team of six and my larger staff of 27 is my second priority. So regular weekly and monthly meetings are scheduled and protected.

Knowing that these large blocks of time are protected from distractions allows me to be more productive during the rest of my week. I don't become stressed out on Tuesday, when I'm busy with staff meetings and administrative demands, because I know that on Wednesday, I'll have my results time.

Response Time

Response time provides blocks of time dedicated to clean-up and follow-up. This is your time to take care of important projects that aren't critical to the mission but still important. As a servant-leader, you'll need to realize that the people you serve have their own agendas and needs. One of their greatest needs is simply to know that you care—that you are there for them. So, you want to be as responsive to them as you can. First you must protect your *rest time* and *results time*, because these are vital to the long term health of the entire organization, business, or church. Once these are covered, the servant-leader should focus his response time on the needs of his team. Response time can generally be defined in this way:

Response time is focused on others—
responding to their needs
and processing the "stuff" that flows from
doing your main thing.

Remember from chapter 1 that "stuff" is the "debris of success." As work or ministry happens, stuff happens and begins to pile up. You may be tempted to try and clean it up, follow it up, a little at a time all day long. This approach lowers the productivity of your results time and ruins the refreshment of your rest time. It's far better to wait until

‹‹‹ ›› ›
Beware of the Little Things

Now let me caution you: Stay focused as you try to do your main thing. It's easy to become distracted by emails, phone calls, unfinished projects, friendly conversations, stacks of unread books and magazines, and all kinds of other interruptions. When these temptations are close by, they're hard to ignore. If you allow yourself to become snared by the distractions, the next thing you know, your whole morning will be gone! You will be much more productive and creative if you tell yourself you must pour all your energies into your main thing during a certain block of time. Even a short distraction of five minutes can be very costly. That's because it will take you at least 20 minutes to get refocused to the same level of creativity and concentration that you had before. So when you work on your main thing, tune out everything else!

your block of response time arrives and do all the clean-up at one time. It's just like picking up trash: You can do it one piece at a time all day long, or you can wait, get the power blower or broom, and go at it. Stuff, like trash, is best swept into a pile and scooped up all at once. You'll get twice as much done in a fraction of the time and enjoy it twice as much! In my schedule, I've set aside three afternoons each week that provide quality time just for responding to our church members, and especially to my leadership team. I process and handle email, phone calls, staff issues, counseling appointments, and whatever else needs my touch. It is a joy to know I have some time set aside just to be available—response time that doesn't intrude into my results time.

Refocus Time

This final "R" is often the most overlooked. People will encourage you to *rest*, demand your *results*, and cry out for your *response*. But they seldom think of your need to *refocus*.

Refocus time is dedicated to working *on* the mission,
not just *in* the mission.
This time is used to assess, adjust,
and innovate for the future.

Because life and leadership are always changing, our responsibilities and priorities, inevitably, are going to shift. Even our unique abilities are under constant refinement, still being discovered and developed as we lead. The very best plan for implementing the four "R's" never works forever. Life is full of surprises. That is the nature of things on planet Earth. So expect to adjust your plan on a regular basis. *Refocus time* is dedicated to making sure these adjustments get made. The main questions you want to ask are:

1. Am I getting the *rest time* I need to stay spiritually healthy and nurture my family or other key relationships?

2. Am I getting quality *results time*, sufficient for advancing the mission and protecting the health of my church or organization? What are my priorities for the coming period of time?

⟨⟨⟨⟩⟩⟩
Beware: "You've Got Mail"

Answering email may not seem such a big deal, but it is. This one activity can rob you of precious time during the most important parts of your day. When it comes to answering email, keep in mind this should fit into the response-time portion of your schedule. Why? Just answer these three questions:

1. Is email on my list of main things? Is answering email what makes this business or ministry hum? Is it God's primary calling for my life?

2. What part of my day am I most creative and sharp? When do I do my best work? Is it morning or afternoon?

3. When do I check and process my email?

I've asked hundreds of leaders to respond verbally to those three questions in my leadership seminars. The vast majority answer them as follows:

1. An enthusiastic, "No! It's not *my* main thing."

2. With exuberant confidence, "Morning!"

3. With sheepish hesitation, "Most days, morning."

Because email is a response-time activity, it shouldn't interfere with your results time or the best part of your day. So resist the temptation to jump every time you see or hear that you have an email waiting to be opened. My suggestion is to answer your emails at the end of your day. You'll be surprised how much faster you process it when you know your spouse and kids are waiting for you to arrive home. "You've got mail" is not nearly as important as that sound at the front door that signals to your family, "You've got home!"

3. Am I structuring and utilizing my *response time* efficiently to care for my team and serve their needs when possible? Am I available to my key leaders?

4. If not, what do I need to do to make the necessary adjustments?

When you use your *refocus time* to break away from your routine to ask God these questions and reflect on your personal life and your profession, you will always get fresh insight that will help you maintain the elusive equilibrium of servant-leadership.

Now, how often should you refocus? Consider these suggestions:

Refocus Weekly. Some refocus time should happen routinely, at the beginning or end of every week. Be honest and ask yourself, "So, how is it going, really?" That's assessment. Am I really resting as I should, maintaining my marriage and family to the glory of God? Am I protecting my prime time for my priorities, my main thing? Am I responding with a servant heart to those who need me most? One to two hours per week of refocus time will deliver results.

Refocus Monthly. Each month, take one day, or at least a morning, to get away from the to-do list and refocus. Pick a regular time each month, and it will bear big dividends. I've told our staff they can take one half-day a month to get away from the office and go to the beach or a park with a lawn chair, a yellow tablet, and their ministry plan. I want them to have time to reflect, dream, listen to God, and refocus. This allows them time to come up with new goals and make adjustments to their personal priorities.

Refocus Annually. At least once a year, go on a retreat for a combination of rest and refocus time. In fact, here's a better idea: Every year, plan *three* retreats. They can be short, but you'll benefit greatly by taking all three retreats so that each one has a single focus:

1. Retreat to Get Ahead—Focus on Your "Main Thing(s)"

Once a year, I go away to a quiet location and spend four to five days planning all my sermons for the coming year. I bury myself in the Scriptures from daybreak into the evening hours. My goal is to come home with 52 sermons selected, titled, and organized for the coming year. This bears great dividends all year long as I approach my weekly preparation, not having to start cold in that week's passage. You can plan a similar retreat to do your big-picture planning and strategizing how to get on top of your main thing.

2. Retreat for Personal Enrichment—Focus on Your Leadership

As a leader, you are constantly giving of yourself to others and your work. If you keep giving out and don't replenish yourself in some way, eventually you're going to become an empty well. It's vital you break away from the everyday grind of leadership and find a place to stretch yourself, learn new ideas, and renew your energy.

3. Retreat with Your Spouse—Focus on Your Relationships

No matter what you do for a living—whether you lead in ministry or in the marketplace—you will be more effective if your marriage is healthy and happy.

I remember sitting in the office of Howard Hendricks—a great role model for leaders—and watching him read a letter he had just received from Coach Tom Landry of the Dallas Cowboys. That year, the Cowboys had gone to the Super Bowl. During that season, Hendricks had offered a marriage-enrichment Bible study for any players and wives who wanted to be involved. In the letter, Landry thanked Dr. Hendricks for all he had done to help the Cowboys achieve their success that season. Landry had observed that the players on his teams who had stable, healthy homes and marriages were always more productive on the field. By contrast, the players who were struggling at home or had turmoil in their marriage were distracted and less likely to experience their full potential.

I believe Landry's observation is applicable to every person, no matter what he or she does for a living. If you have employees who are struggling at home, they will also struggle to some degree at work. I don't care how much you tell someone, "Leave your problems at home; don't bring them to work." Turmoil in the home often spills over and affects everyone—the employee, and all who work alongside him or her. So, if married, take at least one retreat a year and invest in this vital relationship. Make it a weekend just for the two of you—no kids allowed on this one!

The Key to Greater Productivity

Juggling is part of life as a leader. As you juggle well, people will throw more projects your way and the pace will quicken. Some you can ignore, at least for awhile. Some you can delegate to others. And some will need to be juggled only by you. But don't just keep trying to juggle faster. Sop! Look at your workload, and break it down into the four "R's." Ask yourself, "Is there a better way to juggle?" The answer is yes. Concentrate on one kind of activity at a time—whether it be *rest time, results time, response time,* or *refocus time.* You'll find yourself being far more productive, much less stressed, and ready to juggle with a renewed sense of satisfaction and joy.

LESS IS MORE Leadership:
Putting *Concentration—the Power of Focus* into Action

1. Prayerfully determine and name your *main thing(s)*. List up to three items, in order of priority.

2. Write a plan for the flow for **your week** (when and where)...

   • to provide quality *rest time—*

   • to protect your *results time—*

   • for processing the *other stuff* in *response time—*

   • What is your plan for weekly and monthly *refocus time?—*

3. Finally, leaders advance when they *retreat.* So when and where will you go to...

   • nurture your marriage (if married)?

   • be refreshed and enriched professionally?

   • plan your main thing for the coming year?

4. What can you do this year to create a place, free of distraction, to focus on your *main things?*

*"A component of great leadership is
hardiness: resilience, persistence—hope....
Leaders are the purveyors of hope."*[1]
—WARREN BENNIS, USC SCHOOL OF BUSINESS

*"Obstacles cannot crush me. Every obstacle yields to stern resolve.
He who is fixed to a star does not change his mind."*
—LEONARDO DA VINCI

*"We shall overcome, we shall overcome,
We shall overcome—someday."*
—DR. MARTIN LUTHER KING

"We will either find a way or make one."
—HANNIBAL, ANCIENT GENERAL WHO FOUGHT AGAINST THE ROMANS

*"Consider it all joy, my brethren, when you encounter various trials,
knowing that the testing of your faith produces endurance...
that you may be perfect and complete, lacking in nothing."*
—JAMES, ON FACING TOUGH TIMES (JAMES 1:2-4)

CHAPTER NINE

Determination—
The Power of Hope

From time to time, every leader faces circumstances that tempt him or her to despair. These low points usually end up redefining what it means to hit the bottom. Perhaps he or she has been leading to the best of his or her ability but the results are just not happening. There is no assurance that the downward trend is going to reverse itself and head back uphill against the gravity of bad news. Winston Churchill went through such a time during World War II. Hitler was on a roll in Europe and North Africa. The United States was watching from the stands, trying to stay out of the game. Many of Churchill's citizens and associates were starting to lose a leader's most valuable commodity: hope. Churchill, with a tone of determination, spoke:

> We are resolved to destroy Hitler and every vestige of the Nazi regime. From this, nothing will turn us. Nothing! We will never parley. We will never negotiate with Hitler or any of his gang. We shall fight him by land. We shall fight him by sea. We shall fight him in the air. Until, with God's help, we have rid the earth of his shadow.[2]

Determination: An Essential Trait

Determination...resolve...perseverance—this is the eighth component of great leadership. Every business, no matter how good it is, cycles though seasons of drought. Targets are not reached. Results are few and far between. Solutions just aren't. The effort is there, but the effect is an absolute "no show."

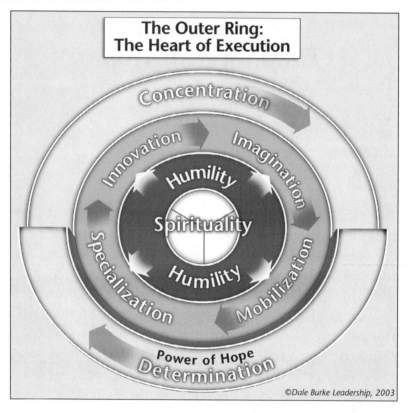

This happens to churches, too. Every church goes through seasons of slow growth or no growth at all. Sometimes you can put your finger on the cause, but it's totally beyond your control. For example, at the first church in which I served as a pastor, a downturn in the economy and a reduction in state funds caused several key leaders to lose their university positions. (The church was in a small Midwest town with a major university as the primary employer.) They ended up having to relocate outside the area. Others who were up for tenure didn't get it, so they soon disappeared. Still others graduated and headed out of town to get jobs. The result? We lost over 60 percent of our leadership base in one summer. What a hit for a church absolutely dependent on a 100 percent volunteer workforce!

Downturns of any kind are frustrating for a leader. You replay your decisions, rethink your strategies, and return to the battle, only to see the next quarter's numbers or attendance keep dropping. At times like these, *determination—the power of hope*—is what keeps you alive. George Washington had it when, several times, it seemed the Revolutionary War would be lost. Abraham Lincoln had it when he lost in eight attempts to be elected to office, yet persevered to become

> ⟨⟨⟨ ⟩⟩⟩
>
> "Success is going from failure to failure without losing enthusiasm."[3]
>
> —Winston Churchill

America's sixteenth president. He drew on hope again during the darkest days of the Civil War and helped preserve a nation. General Douglas MacArthur had it when he said, "I shall return." Jesus Christ modeled it best when He willingly gave up His life on the cross. He knew there was purpose behind His passion and declared with confidence that He would indeed rise again and conquer death itself. Today, His resurrection is not only a fact of history, but the foundation of hope for life beyond the grave.

The *power of hope*—how important is it? Consider this: All of God's commandments are important, but only ten made the short list in Exodus 20. All of God's wisdom should be listened to carefully, but when He later issued an even shorter list on life's essentials, it came down to only three: faith, hope, and love (1 Corinthians 13:33). *Faith* is the basis of any relationship with God, for as Scripture says, "Without faith it is impossible to please Him" (Hebrews 11:6). That is why I place spirituality—the *power of convictions*—as the anchor for all the disciplines in my LESS IS MORE approach to leadership.

Love is the foundation of Jesus Christ's Great Commandment to love God and love others (Matthew 22:37-39)—a two-part commandment that captures the essence of the entire ancient law and prophets of Israel. LESS IS MORE Leadership recognizes that learning to love people is not a "luxury option" in your "leadership package."

It should be standard equipment on every new leadership model. Vibrant spirituality should nurture both faith and love, and produce great servant-leaders who surprise the world with their humility. Faith and love are critical components in the heart of any leader. *Hope* completes God's short list for life as it is meant to be lived. Yet what is its role in leadership?

The determined leader—infused with hope—refuses to say, "I quit." The circumstance may be bad—*really* bad—but don't ever view it as hopeless. When others are resigned to quit, the determined leader's first priority is to restore hope to the team. If hope is kept alive, the team can return to the first seven disciplines and get back on the offensive. Yesterday's path to success may be blocked, and may even seem hopeless, but the good news that *hope* brings is this:

> Yesterday is history;
> today is under way;
> but tomorrow is a whole new day!

There is always hope, a new day for exploring new ways, new products, new services, new untapped resources for getting the job done. Hope is a powerful force—the very foundation of perseverance.

Hope: A Universal Need

Warren Bennis, a highly esteemed professor of business at USC in Los Angeles, the author of over 25 books, a former university president and an advisor to four U.S. presidents, lists the maintenance of hope as a key component in his six competencies of great leadership. Bennis refers to hope as leadership "hardiness" and defines it with words such as *resilience* and *persistence*.[4] So hope is not just for pastoral leaders, it's for every leader.

The power of hope is most clearly seen in the world of sports. A spirit of hope has inspired great comebacks, whereas hopelessness virtually guarantees defeat. One shining example of someone who exhibited hope is John Wooden, the basketball coach at UCLA from 1948 to 1975. Coach Wooden, who is now in his nineties and still sought out as a speaker on issues of life and leadership, is famous for his "Pyramid of Success." Up the left side of his pyramid are five key words: Ambition, Adaptability, Resourcefulness, Fight, and Faith. Success requires a healthy dose of "fight," which Wooden defines with the phrase "determined effort."

Determined effort is exactly what it took for Wooden to achieve the great success he attained. Now considered the premier coach in all NCAA basketball history, he won an amazing ten national championships in his last 12 years before retirement. Most people forget, however, that he won no national titles, not even one, during his first 15 seasons at UCLA. Yes, that's zero. In today's demanding world, with fans and alumni expecting championships all the time, this coach of coaches probably would have never survived 15 years without winning "the big one"! He could have retreated into self-pity and given up the fight to win, but he didn't. Because Coach Wooden persevered, he eventually came to know unparalleled success. With determination and a hopeful spirit he worked to assemble the right staff, the right players, and the right disciplines to win not one, but a string of championships. Replace hope with self-pity, and his story would have a very different ending.

Pessimism: The Gravity of Self-Pity

Self-pity, with its negative and pessimistic spirit, is like organizational gravity. It will always exert a downward pull on your life. Soon, the pessimism of the leader spreads to his team. It quietly makes the rounds, whispering phrases of doubt or despair:

> "This will never work."
> "Oh well, that's just the way it is."
> "I've done all I can do."
> "Until I get more money or staff, it's not going to change."
> "Why should I even try?"
> "I quit."

Negative thinking that is rooted in the soil of self-pity creates a "gravity of hopelessness" that drains the energy of all who fall under its steady, destructive pull. Whether expressed out loud or held deep within, pessimism deflates hope and stops the momentum needed to overcome and tackle the challenge before you. Leaders must be, as Warren Bennis says, "the purveyors of hope."[5] It's part of the job.

Hype vs. Hope: An Honest Look at the Facts

This doesn't mean the leader lives and leads in a dream world and denies reality. He need not, and should not, fear facing the facts. The discipline of determination calls the leader to balance honest assessment with hope-filled vision. He must display both integrity and optimism—facing the hard truth about today while not losing his optimism about tomorrow.

Again, Jesus was the perfect role model when it came to determination. He confronted the brutal facts and told the truth with integrity as He challenged his future leadership team:

I will build my church;
and the gates of Hades will not overpower it (Matthew 16:18).

In the world you [will] have tribulation,
but take courage; I have overcome the world (John 16:33).

> ‹‹ ‹ › ››
>
> "You'll always miss 100 percent of the shots you don't take."
>
> —WAYNE GRETZKY

In essence, Jesus said, "Yes, we will be up against hell itself, but we will overcome. The gates of hell will fall and the church will flourish—in spite of strong opposition. It's going to be a war, but we will win. Now go for it!" Jesus didn't say the Christian life would be easy. He often warned of the hard times ahead for those who followed Him. He told them they would experience real battles against a powerful and evil enemy. Then He assured them, "I will be with you, and the victory will be ours." He infused His followers with real hope.

There is a fine line between the impotency of hype and the power of hope. If the leader provides temporary false hope, he will soon deflate the determination of his team. He will lose credibility. His integrity will be questioned. And his followers will abandon their cause, their leader, or both. Therefore, the determined leader must not only offer optimistic declarations; he must offer real and viable solutions alongside his statements of hope. And if no solution is known, then he must at least set out a course of exploration—with the hope that the solution will soon be discovered.

Hope doesn't just guess; it also does its homework. This too is part of leadership. Before accepting the pastorate at the Evangelical Free Church at Fullerton, I prayed, examined my core values and vision, then proceeded to learn all I could about the church and its history. As I prayed and listened to God, I also asked Him to give me insight and understanding on the pros and cons of this risky move to Southern California. I also sought counsel from those who knew me best and loved me most.

Like any decision in life, ministry, or business, I still had to make the call—to either take a risk or play it safe. The discipline of determination calls the leader not only to resilience, but also to research. If you want your hope to be contagious, to infect the hearts of those following you, then do your homework. Back up your faith with some facts. And then offer hope and go into action.

Hope: The Kind that Never Fails

If a specific hope or dream is based in a promise from God, then you can have complete confidence that it will be fulfilled. For example, the following words of hope and heaven are promised to those whose faith is in Christ as their personal Savior and Lord:

> ...God...has caused us to be born again to a *living hope*
> through the resurrection of Jesus Christ from the dead...
> an inheritance which is imperishable and undefiled
> and will not fade away...reserved in heaven for you,
> who are protected by the power of God... (1 Peter 1:3-5).

Now that is real hope. It is reserved and waiting for us, guaranteed by God's promise and protected by God's power. It is a hope that does not disappoint! (If you as a reader are interested in exploring this hope of eternal life, I would consider it an honor to communicate with you and send you some information on my personal journey to faith in Jesus Christ. After all, that is my "main thing" and my number-one passion! You'll find my contact information in the back of this book.

As a leader, it's vital that you give hope and not hype or empty promises. You must let your people know there is hope, but at the same time, you cannot promise with certainty the precise outcome at the end of the day, or month, or year as you pursue your dreams. Remember, you are not God, so be careful what you promise. Of course, when hope is based on God's promises, our destiny is secure. But when hope is based on man's plans and programs, only time will tell the outcome. In such times, I redirect my personal focus, and the focus of my team, on some "spiritual facts of life" that do not rest on the outcome of our organizational initiatives.

Hope: A Focus for Good Times and Bad

As a Christian, you can be an optimistic leader no matter what trials you face. No matter how bad your circumstances become, you can still have hope. While some or all the people on your team might not share your faith, they can still see and sense the hope it generates in you as their leader. Here are twelve reasons you can be optimistic even in the toughest of times:

A Dozen Reasons to Always Have Hope

God is always with you	Hebrews 13:5
God loves you as His child	Romans 8:15-16
God proved His love at the cross	Romans 8:32
God's power is available to you	Philippians 4:13
God can exceed your highest expectations	Ephesians 3:20
God understands you and your problem	Matthew 6:8
God promises to supply all your needs	Philippians 4:19
God's grace is sufficient for you	2 Corinthians 12:9

God works all things together for good   Romans 8:28
God uses trials to produce maturity   James 1:2-4
God uses trials to display your faith   Philippians 2:15
God's will is good, acceptable, and perfect   Romans 12:2

The promises on this list may not apply to every business situation, but they do apply to every businessman or woman, every leader, every pastor who is a Christian. These promises are the ultimate basis of our optimism and hope. Every leader who is facing a challenge ought to pray through these 12 promises or truths on a regular basis. Give thanks for each of them, in good times or bad! They will restore your joy and resurrect fresh hope every time you make them your focus.

Leaders who exhibit genuine, authentic optimism are a priceless commodity to any organization. And this hope must live *in you,* the leader, if it is to infect those serving *under you.* Professor Howard Hendricks was a master at motivation; he would tell his students, "If you want people to bleed, you have to hemorrhage!" Hemorrhage some hope, and see if your followers don't at least begin to bleed.

> *It is the leader who leads as if God does not exist who is actually living a fantasy.*

Faith and Hope: More Than Mere Positive Thinking

Some skeptics will say, "Faith has no place in leading my business or my team. After all, Dale, I'm not leading a church as you do. I deal in reality, not the fantasies of faith." But when we talk about hope and faith, we're not referring to the empty "power of positive thinking" that smiles while denying reality. Rather, we're talking about bringing reality into focus. As Christians, we know there is a reality beyond what we can see, touch, and measure. We know that God exists, that He loves us, and that His promises can be trusted.

So if you try to assess reality as you face a problem, yet leave God out of the assessment, you will overlook a vitally important part of what is very, very real: God. If you want to confront the "brutal facts" of life, you must also confirm the "spiritual facts" of life: God is alive, able, and aware; and He loves you. Only when you factor this into the equation have you truly defined reality! To exclude the spiritual dimension is to assume a "reality" that does not even exist! Christian faith is not about living in a *fantasy* world, but the *real* world. It is the leader who leads as if God does *not* exist who is actually living a fantasy. His world, void of the spiritual, is not fact at all, but humanistic fiction. It may be politically correct, but it is as incorrect as a spreadsheet with bogus data.

> ⟨ ⟨ ⟨ ⟩ ⟩ ⟩
>
> "The first time I was asked to take a step down in the organization to serve a team that was struggling, I was in conflict. On one hand, I knew that the job aligned well with my strengths and I could be a big help to that team by being their leader. On the other hand, the idea of moving to a lower position in the organization offended me. This went on for a couple of weeks until I got my focus off of myself and onto my team and my Lord."
>
> —A VICE PRESIDENT AT A MAJOR AEROSPACE COMPANY

Warning: Beware of Entitlement Thinking

As we exercise determination, we must make sure we don't slip into an entitlement attitude, often found alongside pessimism and self-pity. It shows itself most clearly in what I like to call "If only..." thinking. For example, you may at times find yourself thinking, *If only someone would do this for me, then I would be able to move forward.* This is the "Poor me, I deserve this, but so-and-so isn't helping" attitude. You assume the role of a victim. You blame someone else for your lack of results, for the difficulty you are having reaching your goals. And you convince yourself that you deserve more than you have and life isn't giving you a fair shake. Don't fall into entitlement thinking; it is a deadly killer of hope.

Hope: Showing It in Action

How does the determined leader foster and maintain hope in others? There are four actions a leader can take to nurture and maintain hope in the face of difficult circumstances. These four actions can be easily remembered by using the word *hope* as an acronym:

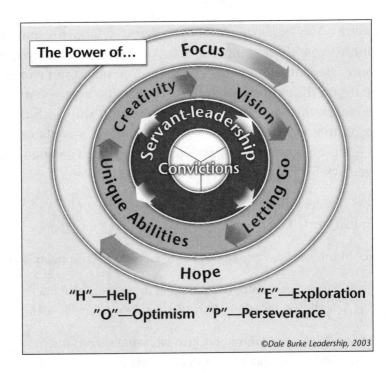

The Power of...   **Focus**

Creativity   *Vision*

Servant-leadership

Convictions

Unique Abilities   *Letting Go*

Hope

"H"—Help   "E"—Exploration
"O"—Optimism "P"—Perseverance

©*Dale Burke Leadership, 2003*

Help!   The leader communicates *compassion*.

Optimism   The leader expresses *confidence*.

Perseverance The leader displays *courage* and *commitment*.

Exploration The leader encourages *creativity*, exploring outside the box.

Help—Great leaders don't just tell others to suck it up and get it done. They first listen and communicate that they care. They show *compassion*—not only for the problem, but for the people who are struggling to solve it. Most people want to make progress. They don't enjoy being stifled or stumped any more than you do. Chances are they've tried their best but need some help. Restoring hope begins by showing your people you understand and care. Leaders must listen, listen, listen. People need your ear before they need your answers. God gave you two ears and one mouth—so listen twice as much as you speak. People follow leaders who listen.

Optimism—The leader must model a positive, hopeful spirit and communicate *confidence* to his team. If you express doubts, you will infect your associates with your pessimism. You might not win every battle, but you should believe every battle can be won. Even if you come to realize the ship is sinking, then abandon ship with the full expectation that it's time for a new ship. If no ship is available, then it's time to trust God and learn to swim! An optimistic Christian leader will never lack for hope if he truly believes God's Word:

> Consider it all joy...when you encounter various trials,
> knowing that the testing of your faith produces endurance (James 1:2-3).

> Rejoice in the Lord always; again I will say, rejoice! (Philippians 4:4).

> Rejoice always; pray without ceasing; in everything give thanks;
> for this is God's will for you in Christ Jesus (I Thessalonians 5:16-18).

> I can do all things through Christ who strengthens me....
> My God will supply all your needs (Philippians 4:13,19).

> All things...work together for good for those who love God,
> to those who are called according to His purpose (Romans 8:28).

Perseverance—The leader with determination is tough and does not quit. He demonstrates *courage* and *commitment* in tangible ways to his followers. They see him take personal risks instead of the safe route. His confidence is matched by the courage to press ahead when others fear the uncertainty or insecurity of the future. He also shows a personal commitment to not abandon ship or desert his troops under fire. He is committed to the cause or goals of the organization and uses his influence and resources to help overcome obstacles.

Exploration—The determined leader doesn't just insist on progress; he is willing to change methods or direction to move the mission forward. He employs *creativity* and searches for a better way to accomplish the goal, even if the old ways were his ways! This leader sees change as a good thing. Leaders who insist on bigger and better results without allowing their team to be innovative will soon see hope deflate.

Remember what we learned in the chapter on the power of vision— a leader must assess, envision, and then adjust because, as we learned earlier, insanity is doing the same thing over and over and expecting different results.

So when the going gets tough, and people are tempted to quit or settle for status quo, determination inspires hope by showing...

Compassion	How can I help?
Confidence	I know we can do it!
Courage and Commitment	Let's never give up!
Creativity	Let's try a new approach!

Resolve: Self-Leadership vs. Self-Pity

We've discussed how easy it is to get discouraged and succumb to self-pity. A good leader, however, sees difficult circumstances as an opportunity to rise to the occasion rather than raise the white flag of defeat. Instead of resorting to self-pity, this leader switches into what I call the self-leadership mode. Self-leadership asks, "What if...?" rather than complaining, "If only...." This leader takes full responsibility for making something happen, in spite of the limitations that surround him. He refuses to take on the victim role and acknowledges his situation without accepting defeat. He says with fresh optimism, "What if..." and again attacks the problem with three liberating assumptions:

〈〈〈〉〉〉

Determination— January 1, 1831

On a plaque outside a church in Newburyport, Massachusetts, are these words, along with the date January 1, 1831:

"I am in earnest,
I will not equivocate,
I will not excuse,
I will not retreat a single inch,
And I will be heard."

—WILLIAM LLOYD GARRISON, A LEADER IN THE MOVEMENT TO ABOLISH SLAVERY IN AMERICA AND PUBLISHER OF *LIBERATOR*

1. *I am free as a leader to get out of the box.* If a particular approach to a problem isn't working, don't keep trying to resolve it the same way. Most leaders have more freedom than they realize.

⟨⟨⟨ ⟩⟩⟩

Exploring the Possibilities

A great example of searching for untapped resources is when our church was working on a plan for a new office structure. We had always struggled with the fact we could easily use more staff but didn't have the money to pay them. When we were adding some new office space, it dawned on me that we could create some volunteer work spaces where people who wanted to help out could be better resourced. We have many gifted people in our congregation who were untapped resources ready to give of their time at no cost. We asked ourselves, "What if we provided a place where they could have their own desk, computer, and telephone, so they could assist an overworked pastor or ministry leader?" So we created several nicely equipped volunteer workplaces. Today, every one of them is now being shared by two, three, or even four volunteers who are devoting hundreds of hours to the ministry of our church. Most of them are doing it at little or no cost, and the new spaces communicated to them that they are valued and loved as part of the team. Now when a pastor comes to me and says, "Dale, for me to move my ministry forward you've got to hire me another assistant," we can give them hope—even if the budget has run dry.

2. *I have resources I've yet to discover.* If you think you've tapped all available resources, look again. There are always untapped or underdeveloped resources around us. Trust me, you still have options available. Look beyond where you've explored in the past.

3. *Challenges are opportunities for innovation.* A challenge can either stop you or stimulate you to find new solutions. Are your challenges stoppers or stimulators? A high percentage of the most creative innovations and many of the greatest success stories in business came about

in response to frustration, or even desperation! It's when we run up against a brick wall that we say, "Maybe there is a better way. If the old way is not working, then what else can I do?" Failure often motivates people to start exploring outside the box.

Determination and Flight 93: The "Let's Roll" Principle

A perfect example of determination in leadership comes from United Airlines Flight 93, which was downed on September 11, 2001, over western Pennsylvania after terrorists hijacked the plane. The phrase "Let's roll" comes from Todd Beamer, who was a passenger on that plane. We will probably never know all the exact details of what happened, but allow me to speculate a bit and imagine how the sequence of events may have unfolded.

We know the terrorists had taken over the flight. They had weapons on them—likely knives—and had already murdered several passengers and crew members. The passengers were probably told to stay in their seats and not to move. No one had weapons, there were no armed guards, and the situation seemed hopeless. There were a lot of people praying hard, praying with passion—that's the first thing we should always do in a crisis. In fact, we know Todd Beamer prayed the Lord's Prayer on a cell phone while talking to an operator.

But Todd and some others did more than just pray. They led with determination. Someone said, "We don't have weapons, but can't we brew hot water? Maybe hot water thrown in the face of a terrorist could serve as a weapon." Someone else could have added, "If we rip off these folding tray tables we've been eating on, we could use them for shields. And the aluminum prongs that come out and curl up could be spears." No one really knows how creative those passengers became under pressure. The point is, these passengers got creative, thought outside of the box, and found resources they didn't know they had. They got organized and came up with a vision, a goal. "What if!" thinking replaced "Oh well" thinking. They found hope and determination. They used their imagination and got innovative and determined, and said, "Maybe we *can* take control of the plane from the terrorists and land it safely. But if nothing else, we can make sure they don't run it into the Capitol or the White House." Again, we don't know the details, but somehow they got organized around a vision, exercised their creativity, focused on their unique abilities, and mobilized for action. With determination they declared, "We're going to do *whatever it takes* to solve this dilemma. Let's go for it." And, as we all know, it was Todd Beamer who, with courage and commitment, said, "Are you guys ready? Let's roll."

Determination looks for the opportunities. It won't take no for an answer.

The people on Flight 93 lost their lives, but they never lost their hope. They took action instead of feeling sorry for themselves. As a result, they became heroes instead of mere victims. Yes, the plane went down. But the passengers went down fighting to the end. The terrorists did not achieve their objective. By the grace of God, these passengers were as creative, as courageous, and as hopeful as they could be, and they will forever be remembered for their determination. Someone on that plane led with the power of hope and the discipline of determination, and others followed.

Determination: The Key to Making a Difference

How determined a leader are you? Scripture encourages us to not just pray when we're faced with an obstacle, but to pray with determination. In Matthew 7:7, Jesus said, "Ask, and it will be given to you; seek, and you will find; knock, and it will be opened to you." This passage, which teaches important principles about prayer, doesn't stop at asking. Jesus encourages the one praying to also seek. Look for the solutions God wants to provide. Jesus said we're to knock on doors and see what opens. He's exhorting us to aggressive, active leadership as we approach the obstacles before us. We as leaders need to get on our knees, pray to God, and stay dependent on Him. But then we are also to seek (open our eyes and start exploring our options) and to knock (on doors to see what might open and who's available). We're to take initiative rather than remain passive. Determination looks for fresh opportunities. It won't take no for an answer. It puts hope in the face of despair—and allows God to bless us in ways we cannot imagine!

So as you lead, keep in mind the story of Flight 93. Whenever you're up against a problem that tempts you to become discouraged or want to quit, exercise the discipline of determination. Unleash the power of hope!

LESS IS MORE Leadership:
Putting *Determination—the Power of Hope* into Action

1. Identify any area in which you are allowing a negative *entitlement attitude* to cause you to think like a victim.

2. Have you allowed pessimism or self-pity to cause you to quit or give up on a goal? When and where?

3. What new or untapped resources could you explore in the coming year to help you break through a barrier?

4. As a leader, evaluate yourself against the four Leadership Actions that stimulate hope:

   Help—Do you show *compassion?*

   Optimism—Do you communicate *confidence?*

   Perseverance—Where are you displaying *courage* and *commitment?*

   Exploration—Are you modeling and encouraging *creativity?*

5. What will you do this year to grow as a "determined leader"?

May We Never Stop Learning

The leaders on Flight 93 will be remembered for years to come as heroes, not victims. They paid the supreme price, made the ultimate sacrifice any leader can make. They deserve to be remembered and honored. Yet I did not write *LESS IS MORE Leadership* for them. This book is for leaders still alive, yet engaged in a very real and daily struggle for life. And far too many are going down, not at the hands of terrorists, but under the pressure of leadership in a world gone out of control. *LESS IS MORE Leadership* is about putting Christian leaders back in control of the plane and restoring their hope for a safe landing. You can lead and still have a life!

Jesus Christ once promised, "I came that they might have life, and have it abundantly" (John 10:10). Later, to His young leaders who would shake up the world, He declared,

> These things I have spoken to you so that My joy may be in you,
> and that your joy may be made full (John 15:11).

I know what it is like to enjoy life and leadership at the same time. Jesus Christ delivers on what He promises. You can lead with a global-sized vision and still have a life! The secret is simple: Lead and live by the same principles modeled by Jesus, and demonstrated by His first-century entrepreneurs. They had no seminary training, no MBAs, no CPAs, and no PhDs...no real experience in leadership at all! Yet they led, and God blessed, and the movement exploded onto the world scene. And they still managed to live and love and have a life at the end of the day.

My passion is to see every leader—paid or volunteer, church board or corporate board—healthy and learning the art of leading with a balanced life. Too many of my pastoral peers have already gone down, and I know the same is true in the business world. No one honors these leaders or celebrates their sacrifice as they slip "down with their ship," or as is more often the case, quietly jump overboard. To these leaders I say, "Come back on board and let's try it again." It's not your fault no one taught you how to lead more and manage less. The LESS IS MORE approach offers leaders who are sinking a chance to dry off, get back on board, and try again. There is always hope!

I want to help lower the casualty rate for leaders and their loved ones. Most leaders are living high-risk lifestyles as they push harder to keep up. Many are already the walking wounded, and have the scars to prove it. I wrote this book for them. I know there is a better way. It is time to quit trying so hard and try "less"! Learn from the one Master and start living to please Him as your CEO—less is more!

Finally, I also wrote this for dreamers like myself—the visionaries who don't want to give up and just settle for "what is." Many of these leaders have been told they could not keep chasing their dreams and expect to have a life at the same time. Not true! You can have your cake and eat it, too. The eight disciplines we've learned—all modeled by Jesus—are based on truth that works anywhere, any time, any place one is called to lead. You and I have far more leadership potential than we know. Let's tap it and grow!

So slow down, and get stable at the core of your life. Dedicate yourself, daily and weekly, to the eight core disciplines of LESS IS MORE leadership.

- Spirituality is the foundation. Make Christ your one Master and listen to His voice, follow His values, and pursue His vision.

- Guard your heart of humility. Remember to be a servant—it's not about you.

- Now pursue the mission with imagination—the power of vision. Don't be afraid to dream new dreams, set new golas, and go for it!

- But remember, you are a limited resource. So mobilize others to lead with you. Let go and continually think, *Lead more, manage less.*

- Now you are free to specialize. Shift more and more of your time into your zone of unique abilities.

- You may be successful, but don't forget that the world around you is changing. Build a culture of innovation, unleash creativity, and never settle for "good enough."

- Finally, tackle your outer ring—continually sharpen you execution. Concentration taps into the power of focus. Structure every week for quality rest time, results time, response time, and refocus time.

- Now lead on with determination, keeping hope alive no matter what! Helpful, Optimistic, Persevering, Exploring. May they be adjectives that defines your leadership. And as life surprises you with seasons of frustration or success...pray and return to the core, the center, and focus on your God, the Lord Jesus Christ, your mentor for all of life.

I know that even as I finish this book, it is the result of a five-year personal journey exploring God's design for leadership and life. Yet I'm still learning. It is painful to release this to the publisher without making just one more change, one more addition. In today's world, we must never stop learning. A friend of mine recently heard Leonard Sweet, author of several books on Christianity and cultural change, make the following observation about life in the twenty-first century:

In the future, everyone will have to *learn* a living.

That might not be true for everyone, but it is certainly true for leaders. May this book not be the end, but the beginning of new lessons learned in leadership for the good of all who follow you and for the glory of the one Master.

Notes

Every Leader's Dilemma

1. Adapted from "Illustration of the Week" by John Ortberg in *Leadership Weekly* (October 3, 2003), at LeadershipJournal.net.

2. Steve and Mary Farrar, *Overcoming Overload* (Sisters, OR: Multnomah Publishers, 2003), p. 11.

Chapter 1—Ten Undeniable Facts for Today's Leaders

1. Peter Drucker, *Post-Capitalist Society* (New York: HarperBusiness, 1993), p. 1.

2. *Newsweek* (May 13, 2002).

3. Jim Collins, *Good to Great* (New York: HarperBusiness, 2001).

4. Ronald Heifetz and Donald Laurie, "The Work of Leadership," *Harvard Business Review*, December 2001.

Chapter 2—Spirituality

1. Jim Collins and Jerry Porras, *Built to Last: Successful Habits of Visionary Companies.* (New York: HarperInformation, 1997).

2. Jim Collins, at a conference in Colorado Springs in 1997. Collins also addresses this at greater length in his book *Built to Last* on p. 75.

3. John Bradley and Jay Carty, *Discovering Your Natural Talents* (Colorado Springs: NavPress, 1991), p. 25.

4. Dale Burke, *A Love That Never Fails* (Chicago, IL: Moody Press, 1999).

Chapter 3—Humility

1. Jim Collins, *Good to Great* (New York: HarperBusiness, 2001), pp. 12-13.

2. Ken Blanchard, *Convene* (February 1998), p. 75.

3. Collins, *Good to Great*, pp. 12-13.

4. "If It Ain't Broke, Break It!" *Sports Illustrated* (April 14, 1986), p. 52.

Chapter 4—Imagination

1. Robert Kriegel and Louis Patler, *If It Ain't Broke...Break It!* (New York: Warner Books, 1992), p. 35.

2. Bill Hybels, "Five Things Leaders Do," an article posted on BuildingChurchLeaders.com, ©2003 by Christianity Today International/ *Leadership Journal,* September 9, 2003.

3. Ronald Heifetz and Donald Laurie, "The Work of Leadership" *Harvard Business Review* (December 2001), p. 131.

Chapter 5—Mobilization

1. John Kotter, "What Leaders Really Do," *Harvard Business Review* (December 2001), p. 85.

2. Walter Bruckart as cited by Jim Collins, *Good to Great* (New York: HarperBusiness, 2001), p. 55.

3. As cited by Jim Collins, *Good to Great*, p. 55.

4. As cited by Steve Miller, *D.L. Moody on Spiritual Leadership* (Chicago: Moody Publishers, 2004), p. 179.

5. John Kotter, "What Leaders Really Do," p. 85.

6. Warren Bennis and Robert Thomas, *Geeks and Geezers: How Era, Values, and Defining Moments Shape Leaders* (Boston, MA: Harvard Business School Press, 2002), p. 137.

Chapter 6—Specialization

1. Marcus Buckingham and Donald O. Clifton, *Now, Discover Your Strengths* (New York: Simon & Schuster, 2001), p. 6.

2. Jim Seybert, a brainstorm and ideation consultant, in an email to the author on March 3, 2004.

3. John Bradley and Jay Carty, *Discovering Your Natural Talents* (Colorado Springs: NavPress, 1991), p. 17.

4. Buckingham and Clifton, *Now, Discover Your Strengths*.

5. Bradley and Carty, *Discovering Your Natural Talents*.

Chapter 7—Innovation

1. As cited on the Cambridge Philosophy Institute Website at www.cambridgeuni.org.uk/pressmessage.html.

2. As cited by Robert Kriegel and Louis Patler in *If It Ain't Broke...Break It!* (New York: Warner Books, 1992), p. 78.

3. Gordon MacKenzie, *Orbiting the Giant Hairball* (New York: Viking Press, 1996), p. 97.

4. Jim Collins, *Good to Great* (New York: HarperBusiness, 2001), pp. 1, 16.

5. Kriegel and Patler, *If It Ain't Broke...Break It!*, p. xvi.

6. From a speech to the American Electronics Association on September 28, 1988; as cited in Kriegel and Patler, *If It Ain't Broke...Break It!*, p. 112.

7. Kriegel and Patler, *If It Ain't Broke... Break it!*, p. 69.

8. Margaret Wheatley, as stated at the Innovation Network Conference in Minneapolis on September 22, 2002; as cited on the Leadership Network website at www.leadnet.org/allthingsIn/archive_template.asp?archive_id=848db=explorer

9. MacKenzie, *Orbiting the Giant Hairball*, p. 32 (emphasis added).

10. MacKenzie, *Orbiting the Giant Hairball*, p. 33.

11. Howard Shultz to Warren Bennis at a LeadershipTraq banquet on January 22, 2004.

12. Jim Seybert, *Market Intelligence*, March 2004, used with permission.

13. MacKenzie, *Orbiting the Giant Hairball*, p. 97.

Chapter 8—Concentration

1. Peter Drucker, *The Effective Executive* (New York: HarperBusiness, 1966), p. 25.
2. The general approach to managing time in large blocks was first presented to me in an excellant booklet by Dan Sullivan, *How the Best Get Better* (Toronto, Canada: Strategic Coach, Inc., 1996).
3. Drucker, *The Effective Executive*, p. 48.
4. Alex MacKenzie and Ted Engstrom, *Managing Your Time* (Grand Rapids, MI: Zondervan, 1967), p. 53.

Chapter 9—Determination

1. Confucius, as cited by Warren Bennis of the USC School of Business at a LeadershipTraq event on January 21, 2004.
2. Winston S. Churchill, *The Grand Alliance* (Boston: Houghton Mifflin, 1950), p. 371.
3. As cited on www.cyber-nation.com.
4. As cited by Warren Bennis at LeadershipTraq on January 21, 2004.
5. As cited on www.cyber-nation.com.
6. Bennis quoting Confucius.

To contact the author, write:

Dale Burke
℅ Harvest House Publishers
990 Owen Loop North
Eugene, OR 97402

You can also find out more
about the LESS IS MORE Leadership
seminars at www.daleburke.com